'If a genius is someone whose ideas survive all attempts at explanation, then by that definition Stockhausen is the nearest thing to Beethoven this century has produced. Reason? His music lasts. The early works still scintillate. They have not become fashions because they have not been successfully copied, and no-one has copied them successfully because no-one else has adequately sussed them out. Nevertheless, like great vintages, their attractive qualities are now beginning to reveal themselves more clearly with the passage of time, as performers and audiences alike become more attuned to the aesthetic of the 1950s and 1960s, not to mention disenchanted with the rapidly fading efforts of younger generations.

The other proof of genius is a continued ability to provoke. As long as I have known Stockhausen, there have always been critics and associates panning the latest composition. It's always the latest work, never the last-but-one. In 1964 the latest composition was a full-length piece for solo tam-tam and six players, *Mikrophonie I*. People were appalled at the idea of making an entire piece out of a single tam-tam (well, yes, with a couple of microphones, filters, etc.). And yet today I can't hear a dog bark in the street without knowing exactly how that sound can be reproduced using a plastic ice-cream box scraped down the tam-tam surface. In 1968 the latest composition was *Stimmung*, a ritual for six voices based on a single chord. Boulez said "how typically German, the endless chord". Stravinsky was said to remark that it called for the musical equivalent of a parking meter. In Holland, a performance caused a near-riot. Judge for yourself whether they, or composers John Tavener and Jonathan Harvey, for whom *Stimmung* is a major source of spiritual inspiration, are right.'

Robin Maconie, Classic CD
September 1990

'Stockhausen's uncompromising attitude to conventional aesthetics has made him one of the world's most admired musicians.'   *The Independent*

'His mastery of the musical possibilities opened up by electronic synthesis has proved as fruitfully influential as anything in post-war composition . . . it is Stockhausen who understands the territory and is marking out its uncharted boundaries.' *Rupert Christiensen, Sunday Times*

'Let there be no doubt that he is a giant, a monster cartographer of massive new spaces.'   *Tempo*

'Maconie successfully elicits a series of fascinating responses from the composer on subjects as diverse as electronics and music teaching . . . they always make for compelling reading.'   *Nicholas Williams, Classical Music*

STOCKHAUSEN
ON MUSIC

STOCKHAUSEN ON MUSIC
Karlheinz Stockhausen

Lectures and Interviews compiled by
Robin Maconie

MARION BOYARS
LONDON • NEW YORK

First paperback published in Great Britain and the United States 1991
by MARION BOYARS PUBLISHERS LTD
24 Lacy Road, London SW15 1NL

www.marionboyars.co.uk

Distributed in Australia and New Zealand by Peribo Pty Ltd,
58 Beamount Road, Kuring-gai, NSW 2080

Reprinted in 2000
10 9 8 7 6 5 4 3 2 1

Originally published in hardcover in 1989 by Marion Boyars Publishers
© Karlheinz Stockhausen 1989
© Compilation Robin Maconie 1989

A CIP catalogue record for this book
is available from the British Library

A CIP catalog record for this book
is available from the Library of Congress

ISBN 978-0-7412-2918-9

Typeset in 11.5/13.5 Baskerville and Helvetica by Ann Buchan
(Typesetters), Shepperton
Printed and bound in Great Britain by Athenaeum Press,
Tyne & Wear

CONTENTS

PART 1

PART 2

Appendices

ACKNOWLEDGEMENTS

I am indebted to Karlheinz Stockhausen for his unstinting cooperation and support in compiling this volume. I am also most grateful to Robert Slotover of Allied Artists, London, on whose initiative the films of Stockhausen's 1971 lectures were made, for access to, and permission to use transcriptions of these lectures and of an informal interview from the same year. Additional thanks to Anthony Mulgan, Gwyneth, Kathryn and Alys for easing the work process in their several ways, and to Marion Boyars for showing uncommon patience.

Robin Maconie

INTRODUCTION
by Robin Maconie

In 1971 Stockhausen visited Britain for a season of public concerts and lectures. He was in buoyant and communicative mood. MANTRA, his newest work, written for two pianos and electronic modulation, marked the end of a particularly difficult period of introspection and a return to a style combining classical energy and discipline with a restrained and theoretically brilliant use of sophisticated electronics. His lectures were a remarkable achievement, addressing the most difficult and hitherto esoteric topics of contemporary music in layman's language before a substantially non-specialist public. Their publication is long overdue, and it is thanks to the fact that many were preserved on film by Robert Slotover, that the present edited transcripts, approved by Stockhausen, can now be made available to a wider readership.

Like all of the material in the present volume, the lectures were given in English, often with impromptu additions. I have tried as far as possible to ensure that the flavour of Stockhausen's English and the informal atmosphere of the lecture theatre are retained. (The lecture 'Four Criteria of Electronic Music', for example, is very different from the German version published in Wulf Herzogenrath (ed.): *Selbstdarstellung: Künstler über sich*, Droste Verlag, Düsseldorf, 1973.) For those interested in the personality of a great composer they constitute a uniquely accessible self-portrait. For working musicians, composers, students and teachers of new music, on the other hand, they have a deeper significance. Since 1950 the world of music has faced an enormous challenge: to discover a rational and objective theory of music to replace the limited and inadequate framework of conventional tonality. It was acknowledged that any new theory of music would have to encompass cultural and theoretical extremes, European and non-European, written and oral, existing or foreseeable. Among the generation of post-war composers faced with this challenge, none is better qualified than Stockhausen to articulate the philosophical and practical issues underlying avant-garde music; it is his extraordinary achievement to have demonstrated, both in his writings and in his compositions, that the theoretical basis of the new music — whether it be serial, electronic, statistical or indeterminate — can be shown to be powerful, rational, coherent, and universal.

Today's listeners and musicians are increasingly attuned to new technologies of the eighties. Digital audio and surround-sound are bringing a clarity and realism to music reproduction which is already changing the listening habits and sharpening the musical and technical perceptions of the general public, proving that the more you are able to hear, the better you do hear, and the more sophisticated a listener you become. Similarly the arrival of the domestic microprocessor, not to mention MIDI and sound sampling technology, has brought electronic music synthesis to the practical attention of an entirely new culture of computer programmers and games enthusiasts.

For the new generations educated by the technology of the market place, bypassing the educational system, traditional music theory and aesthetics are blinding irrelevancies. What they need are descriptive tools for synthesis and composition which correspond to the structures and language of computer programming. They will find Stockhausen an invaluable guide, step by step, from point music to groups, from groups to statistical masses, to mobile form, to process composition, to the construction and derivation of musical formulas. Popular technology has finally caught up with the concepts of that remarkable post-war musical renaissance. A popular culture rooted in new technology has the vitality and the means to pursue Stockhausen's musical researches: it remains to be seen whether it will develop the motivation.

Stockhausen's lectures are amplified and brought closer to date with a series of questions and answers recorded in 1981, in which I sought to draw him on a number of practical and slightly more technical issues. His observations on studio practice will be of particular interest to composers and sound engineers. I would like to think his prescriptions for the synthesizer and home listening environment of the future might stimulate the development of suitable prototypes. What he has to say about composing and production of music theatre in the round should be required reading for producers of television and video music presentations. Last but not least, Stockhausen's prescription for music education has, I believe, enormous relevance both now and for the future.

PART 1

ABOUT MY CHILDHOOD

*From an informal conversation
with an anonymous interviewer, London 1971*

I come from a family of farmers. My father came from a family of very poor farmers, my mother as well. My father was the first in his family to become an intellectual, so to speak. He trained for a short time after the first world war and became a schoolteacher. He used to tell me how he had to walk to the station for more than an hour, put his dirty shoes behind a tree, change his pants quickly and comb his hair, then jump on the train and go to the school. That made a great impression on me.

I have always had very good health. I have an excellent body. It comes from the fact that I had to do physical work from childhood. From three or four years old, I was working all the time, in the garden, or running and collecting the contributions my father had to get for the party and other associations, which was a job a schoolteacher had to do in the Third Reich. There were three or four different collections every month. One collection was said to be for German folk in foreign countries, one was for the *Winterhilfe*, to support the poor in winter. But it was all going toward the build-up of an enormous national power, to the army, and to the youth organizations, and so on. The schoolteachers had the role of collecting the money, and I was the one who had to do it in our area, since my father was also working as a labourer to make some more money because we were very poor.

There was music in the family. My father played the piano: he was self-taught, and played only the black keys, but the sound was fantastic, I found it extraordinary. Perhaps he did play white keys every once in a while, but he was basically a black-keys player. And he played violin fairly well. My mother must have been exceptionally talented musically; I learned from her brothers and sisters that she had privileges that nobody else in her family had. She was excused going to work in the fields and allowed to stay at home. They bought a piano for her: imagine what that means.

I remember being carried on my father's back in about my second year, when he went hunting, riding on a bicycle. Sometimes he would put the catch in the back pack with me, other times I used to sleep outdoors, next to my dog. Another vivid memory is of a small airplane coming down in a field right in front of our house, because of fog. At one time, when I can't have been much more than three years old, I used to explore a cemetery which was fairly close to our house, and I remember seeing an enormous elephant walking in the river nearby. My father made me play tricks on our visitors, for fun. I would put a frog in my pocket and bring it out and frighten the guests. Another trick was to have a worm on my tongue, so that when a stranger said hello I would open my mouth, and they would see the worm and scream. Later, at six or seven, I would astonish people by listening to a tune just once on the radio, then sit at the piano and play it back immediately, with all the right harmonies. It was nothing I had to work at, simply a talent I had.

My mother was taken away when I was four, to a hospital for mentally depressed people. She had a nervous breakdown after having borne three children in three years of poverty. From then on my father's life was a perpetual struggle, worrying over the most banal details of family life. I remember how often we had to move house. Being a young teacher, my father used to stay perhaps half a year at a time in one place, then would be ordered to go to another school. We moved house four times in the four years till I was five, then came to Altenberg, where we stayed until he enlisted and went to the war.

As the village schoolmaster my father was at the centre of village life, but at the same time he was also under the control of the Gestapo, and often found himself in situations of emotional conflict. There were three notorious leftists in the village with whom he was friendly; God knows, they were real primitives, of a peasant mentality, always getting into trouble and being put in jail. They tried to blow up the cathedral in Altenberg, a most beautiful 12th-century Gothic cathedral, just to prove their political beliefs. The bomb went off, but didn't destroy it. They were caught, and put in jail for a long time, finally ending up in concentration camps. My father helped some of these people when they were hiding from the police.

On another occasion the bishop came to visit the village, and I recited a poem, which my father had helped me write, as the bishop entered the village. The poem included two lines at the end, which went as I remember:

> Though the storms of unbelief and destruction rage still more strongly than they do now, yet we will hold up our faith.

I was ten years old, very idealistic, and I remember asking him to help me formulate these last two lines. The next day the Gestapo came and took him away from home, and accused him of putting those words into my mouth. I remember him coming home, completely pale, and he said, if you ever say a word that I had anything to do with it, I will kill you. You have to say you did it all on your own. I said, that's okay: I could see he was in trouble.

He left the church, though he continued to pray every morning. In 1938 he married again; God knows why. He had no money, being paid the equivalent of thirty pounds a month, so not being able to find anyone else he took a succession of peasant girls as housekeepers to cook and to take care of my sister and myself. These girls were notoriously dullwitted and very neurotic. I think he married just to solve the problem of having someone in the house, because otherwise she would have left after three months, like all the rest.

At ten years old I was put into an *Oberschule* in Burscheid. I was there until the age of twelve. It was a high school, what we in Germany call a neo-humanistic grammar school. Before that my father tried to put me into a political high school, for which you were selected on the basis of intelligence and physical condition, and also your family. I know my father went to great pains to discover every root and branch of the family, to as far back as the Thirty Years' War in the seventeenth century. They were all farmers: on my mother's side as well, all farming stock. That was important. I remember my father was very proud. But because of my mother's illness I was not accepted in this élitist school, so I stayed in the *Oberschule*.

My father had a compulsion to get away and enlist. At the time of the Czechoslovakian crisis, he volunteered for the air force; then after the crisis was over and he was released, he volunteered again in '39 when it all started again in Poland. I couldn't understand, I said, why do you go? It's ridiculous, stay here. He said, no, no, I have to go, I'm needed there.

Somehow I think he just wanted to die. My father had talent and it was unrealized. Somehow he was caught up by the national pride that had taken over all those in humble positions. He really believed in what he was doing, in fighting, as before the war he really believed that what was happening was for the good of Germany.

In January 1942 I was put into a national academy for training teachers. It was complete isolation, everything militaristic, uniform, no civilian conditions. Two hours free a week to go into town. Sports, sports and more sports – and three orchestras, very nice orchestras actually, a good jazz band, a symphony orchestra and a salon orchestra, which played light music. I played several instruments. The training was very tough. You got up with the trumpet call at six o'clock, and you went to bed with the trumpet exactly at ten every evening. The whole day was completely organized; there was not a single hour left unaccounted for in the collective schedule. After getting up you did your early morning run, then there were meetings where we assembled in the square to hear the daily curriculum and the news about the war, all of it ideologically coloured. After that, breakfast; every third week it would be your turn to serve your group breakfast and meals at table for three days, on a rota. In the first year you were twenty-five to a room, in the second year sixteen, the third year six to eight, and the fourth year only three or four. And everything was organized; you were always controlled. Every tooth, every fingernail controlled: you had no privacy, and you were never alone.

How much this affected me is impossible to say. I have always been an organized person. It's in my blood. It's very easy for me and it comes quite naturally. Other people don't find it so easy. I make decisions very quickly. I have to be very organized in my life because I do so many things at once, and many people depend on me, and I have to be always on the alert for things that might go wrong.

I lost both of my parents in the war. I was thirteen, and on special vacation from college because my father was on leave from the army, when I learned that my mother had been officially put to death. There was a law during the war that these people could be killed because they were just useless, and because their food was needed. My mother was said to have died of leukaemia; we were told we could have the ashes, which we found quite unusual as we were a Catholic family. But I understood that everybody who died at that hospital was supposed to have died from the same illness. The authorities just didn't want to leave any trace. My father showed me the letter saying my mother was dead and did we want the ashes, and he said, what shall we do? If we take the ashes, what shall we do with them? I remember I was not very shocked at the time; I simply accepted it as given, not as an injustice, a challenge, that's my way.

In 1944 everybody else in my class was called up for army service. They weren't called classes, we were divided up into platoons like in the army, about twenty-five to each platoon. I was two or three years younger than the others in my platoon, because I had been to high school and had already trained in Latin and English and mathematics. So they put me into an older platoon, where I was also the smallest, always at the back when we were on parade – and it made boxing very difficult as well! So when the others were all called up, only two of us were left, one because he wasn't accepted by the army, and me. First I was put into a youth organization that had to build the famous west wall against the approaching armies of the English and the Americans. After that I had to serve for seven months in a war hospital, right behind the line, helping and taking care of the heavily wounded who would arrive untreated direct from the battlefront.

That was an unforgettable experience: to see thousands of people badly wounded and dying, day after day. At night we had to put them on trains, as long as the bombers were not too aggressive. I can see images of it even now. But it was also a wonderful political education, the best training in how to see through all the political ideologies that are used to inflame one people against another. For the first time in my life I had the chance to talk to English and Americans who were wounded. They were frightened out of their wits that they would be killed by the Germans because they had been brainwashed into believing that they would be tortured to death if they fell into German hands. They were trembling, these 20, 22, 23 year-old guys, and they confided in me because I was still younger than them, and I was the only one in the hospital who spoke English. I have an aptitude for languages, and was fluent in English, so I had to translate for them and ask the dying what they wanted. And they saw that this was all so relative, and how the German soldiers really behaved.

When it became clear that the war was lost, the decline in human morality took me by surprise. Morals no longer meant anything. I learned that death was nothing I would ever be afraid of. Several times I came close to dying. I saw that when people are determined to win, as the Americans and English were then, they wouldn't hesitate to choose the most inhuman methods to win by. There was an enormous red cross painted on the roof of our building, clearly visible from the air, but they had no problem in shooting at it, right into the wounded, every day, and dropping phosphate afterwards. It became very clear to me that people acting collectively on a large scale could become completely impersonal and unconcerned, caring only to win, that's all.

But I also made the interesting discovery that I could play music in all styles, and when the soldiers were especially depressed and down at heart, they would always ask me to play for them. There was an old piano in the hospital, and I would play for them. When everything else was gone, music seemed to be of value. There was always food available, they weren't lacking for that, but it was when they felt their lives no longer had any meaning that they liked to have me play for them. I would play for hours, to suit all tastes. One would ask for a Beethoven sonata and another for a very vulgar song, or a sentimental ballad. All kinds. They liked it very much.

My father was shot in battle. I last saw him in 1945, for about three days. I was not quite seventeen. It was April 1945, just before the end of the war. Imagine, during the war I saw him three times, perhaps. He didn't want to come back after the war. He told me he wanted to die. I think he could imagine what really would have happened after the war, if he had returned. I was told by other people in our village that he would have had at least four or five years of agonizing terror; he would have been taken away from home by the Americans and English, and accused of political activity just for being a member of the party, a block leader responsible in the village for collecting party dues. I remember he always said, you see, I have done what I could do. The last time I saw him, he said, I won't come back, now take care of yourself.

The more that was taken away from me the stronger I became. I think, because of that, I have a very special relationship to my parents. I have never been angry or critical about them, as some people say. I think that, being dead, they gave me much more support than they would have in life.

ON THE MUSICAL GIFT

*From an informal conversation
with an anonymous interviewer, London 1971*

People think that if you have two ears you have the same right as anybody else to make judgements about music. That is not true at all. Being musical is something very special, which is recognized even among families who have no special training, when the father and mother can say a child is very musical, because he can immediately pick up a tune and sing it, whereas other children can't. Or whenever he gets an instrument in his hand he does something meaningful with it, so that it begins to sound, whereas the others have no talent whatsoever.

The idea that all music is for everybody is equally ridiculous. People can be influenced by all music, of course: that is natural. But certain people simply respond to sounds far better than most.

I never thought of myself as exceptionally gifted. Comparing my own work with that of my colleagues, I think I have just worked very hard all the time, and that my special talent of always trying to explore new possibilities and enlarge our consciousness seems to be more needed at the present time than being able to convince people of one's genius as a fantastic performer or composer of music in an established style. We are living in a time when the number of people who are extraordinarily devoted to their talent is decreasing, and I see everywhere that there is less place in present-day society for those of extraordinary talent, because of the general tendency to level off the peaks and make everyone equal, and not accept that there are natural differences among people. It's completely absurd to be in a social situation where you feel obliged to defend yourself for what you are.

I respond to sounds. Directly. Sound is my air. Whenever I deal with sounds, they organize themselves, so to speak. They respond very well to me and I to them. When a sound comes into my fingers in the studio or anywhere else, I can immediately place it in an environment of sounds. I have intuitive visions of sound-worlds, music, and a great pleasure in sitting down and writing the music, that's all. And I see some of my colleagues, and they simply can't sit still for more than a few hours without needing a coffee or to do something else. My greatest pleasure is to sit for ten or twelve hours and compose, or work in the studio. It's marvellous.

Our whole tradition is visual: our intellect, our senses, are trained to respond to visual information. Our concepts are visual, the words we use to describe them are visual. We haven't even words to describe sounds, or very few, that are not visual in what they express. People speak of sounds as going up or going down, talk about a big sound, describe tone colours as bright or dark. We are no longer, have long ceased to be in fact, an aural society, one which communicates mainly by hearing. Our entire system of values, of the things we accept to be true, is based on the visual sense. You have to sign a paper because your word is not enough to be trusted.

As a result the acoustic faculty in human beings has declined. So that, for example, we find everybody talking now about the design of the environment, the design of furniture, of clothing, and so on. People are now able to respond to the visual world in a more artistic way. In the years since the war there has been a boom in environmental design: every window or advertisement now has learned a lot from Mondrian. But the acoustic environment, on the other hand, the sounds that occur on the streets, are just taken for granted. If the visual world were as full of garbage as the acoustic world is full of acoustic garbage, the public would be protesting all the time. It obviously goes to show that most people are acoustically deaf, incapable of noticing the acoustic pollution of the world, which is far more critical than the visual pollution.

Actually, television and sound recordings will bring about a new balance between the aural and the visual. I think that more and more poetry will be created which is meaningful as sound rather than in the literal sense. Now tape machines are in many homes, and more and more people listen to recorded sounds. The telephone has also changed things a lot, by giving people the possibility of speaking to each other instead of writing.

I want to build a new tradition, an aural tradition, transmitted via the ears. I feel a duty to perform my music, and I have played all over the world. Then there are my recordings. I consider a record I make as important as the score. Many of them contain music which is not determinate. So the records are models for musicians. The musicians can refer to these recordings and learn from them, and develop their own new approaches to creating sound worlds.

This new aural tradition which I have started means that our musical knowledge will come to be based more and more on direct experience of working with sounds, rather than on writing on paper. New possibilities are discovered and can develop so much faster, when someone works in a studio and produces the sounds himself, and transforms them. Many musicians today know a lot about recording techniques and they penetrate right into the sound, using transforming devices, synthesizers, filters, modulators, dynamic controls, all of which make it possible to live with the sound to a far greater extent than has been the case for a long time in our musical tradition.

We know that during the baroque period, a composer like Bach worked very closely with musicians, and could immediately try out with them what he was working on, and then correct his scores. He could even leave quite a lot to the musicians, give only basic indications, and they would know what he intended and fill out the part accordingly. This close working relationship with musicians is even more necessary nowadays, now that timbre is involved, and movement of sound in the auditorium space has become very important. Such things can only be achieved by experiment and afterwards written down in more or less definite form for use in subsequent performances. It leads to a situation where you can no longer treat the materials of music as separate from the process of composition. The material and the forming of the material become united. I think that's a very positive development.

It means, first of all, that the work of art is no longer a dead object, as it has increasingly become in our culture, something to be traded from place to place, a musical score to be executed, the highest interpretation of which is taken to be when a performer exactly follows the instructions on the printed page. In fact, that is only one aspect of creativity. Much more interesting is the response of a performer to a work determined by what I call 'process planning'. I started process planning in the early fifties, not later than 1955, which were plans for musical processes allowing for many different realizations, though all sharing a basic generic similarity. Such musical works of mine become living beings capable of developing in many different ways, but preserving a common integrity, which is given in the rules which govern the process.

Openness of the musical process is one thing, the other is openness of material as well. The instrumentation is no longer defined once and for all, for instance as 'a piece for oboe, piano and cello'. Rather, the work is relatively defined so that it may be played with any instruments, any sound sources of the future, defining instead the relationships between timbres in a qualitative way, and not in terms of the objects which have to be used to produce the sounds. Again, the number of people participating in certain processes should not be absolutely but relatively determined, so that the music may be performed on different occasions under different circumstances.

Everything that is determined once and for ever is like an order: you either submit to it or go against it, in which case you make a mistake. The alternative is a multi-meaningful order, with which you might feel free to use your imagination, in order really to interpret the instructions that are given. The openness should be open for all time and for all sorts of human minds. Ultimately – this is the final stage – these works should be open to intuition. The more that is determined in a musical work, the more transformations intervene in the process of interpretation. You have to read the score, you have to transform what you read into action, you have to adjust your action to certain pre-determined techniques of making the instrument sound, and so on. But the less determined these details are, and the more direct the way of describing the music in intuitive terms is, the fewer transformations there are to take place. Normally the journey from the composer to the sound is very long; it can take several months for something written by a composer to become sound, because the performer is involved in weeks and weeks of rehearsal and experiment before he can get it right.

Intuitive music, as the word says, comes from intuition. Intuition, for me, is a higher level of consciousness above and beyond the mental. It can be contacted at any instant, not 'higher up' in space, but in its own region of the cosmos. It has a particular structure: there is the level of illumination which we attain only for brief moments, then there are two more, before you reach the level of total consciousness where everything becomes clear. Intuition is always present, as a source. When I speak of intuitive music I don't mean music which arises from memory or the subconscious, but definitely from an influence from the outer to the inner.

I could not receive any exceptional flash of intuition, going beyond what I know or what might be deduced from what I know of the past, if there were not a constant stream of new influences on me, coming from all of humanity and its achievements, and the interferences of their vibrations. And equally, influences from outer space, from the stars and centres of energy that emit waves that are structured in a particular way. When I compose I become aware of the fact that the most important creative insights are those I cannot explain. Even with the sharpest intellectual training, they remain inexplicable. For example, I have dreamt a piece and then written it as I dreamed it; any exact psychological analysis would simply reduce this fact to another fact and then to a third fact, which doesn't lead us anywhere. It's a chain of reasoning which simply peters out. Surely it is far more realistic to live with the daily experience that there is always a completely organized and spiritual activity working upon me and through me, and what is more important than anything else is that I should be able to formulate it, materialize it, whatever it might be, in words or action or in making music. Ultimately, I would say that all music, or more specifically all the new music that takes us further, is already there in the intuitive domain.

Of course there is a seemingly new music which can be made by intellectual variation of what has already been done and experienced. Some of it can even be widely accepted as intelligent and good music. If you have a strong brain, combinatory skills, or even a computer to go beyond the combinatory abilities of the human brain, you can do stunning things, enlarging the circle of variation to a point where you break into completely new experiences. But it remains essentially a music based on the principle of variation of what is already known.

When I speak about receiving vibrations, I am referring to the simple banality that everybody experiences a constant bombardment of rays from the cosmos. Everyone can tell the difference between a sunny or a cloudy day. But in our society, the science of these vibrations is at a very primitive level at the present time. People consider these vibrations as neutral, lacking in identifiable character or quality, as being all the same, which is ridiculous. If there is a spring flowing under your house, you soon know the effect it has on the human psyche.

Being musical has to do with intuitive intelligence, not just communicatory intelligence. The centre of communicatory intelligence in man, the second centre, is where the vocal chords are. Normally the voice is not well coordinated with the rest of the body. I would say that the people I have met who are very musical are those who have a particularly good relationship between their mental and vocal centres. The ear is not a centre, only an organ, a microphone.

The artist has long been regarded as an individual who reflected the spirit of his time. I think there have always been different kinds of artists: those who were mainly mirrors of their time, and then a very few who had a visionary power, whom the Greeks called augurs: those who were able to announce the next stage in the development of mankind, really listen into the future, and through their work prepare the people for what was to come. Only a very few artists in each epoch have had this talent. Today the artist is obliged to take this role, and take it much more seriously than ever, because what is coming is just unbelievable for most human beings.

Musical training has nothing to do with musicality. You can train someone for years in a conservatoire of music and develop the ability to recognize pitch constructions, harmonies, chords, melodies, intervals — all intellectually. But what I call a musical person is someone who can imitate any sound that he hears, with his voice, directly, without thinking about hitting the right pitch, but just doing it. And not only imitating the pitch, but the timbre as well. Great musicians always start off as great imitators. Afterwards, building on the talent of imitation, comes the talent to transform what you hear. Many don't reach that far, but those who attain the ability to transform, incorporate and identify sounds, they are the better musicians. Then comes the last stage of perfecting this ability so that it becomes almost automatic. Nowadays I know immediately, when I hear any sound of nature or traffic, how to synthesize it, and I know many who have tried very hard, and failed, because they don't have the natural faculties for analysis and imitation in the system.

It is very important that the breakthroughs in our time go beyond all the limits that we have accepted up to now. People usually think that the arts should only entertain, but that is not the role of the arts at all. The role of the arts is to explore the inner space of man; to find out how much and how intensely he can vibrate, through sound, through what he hears, whichever it is. They are a means by which to expand his inner universe.

POINTS AND GROUPS

From the lecture MUSICAL FORMING
*filmed by Allied Artists, London, 1971,
and from an informal conversation
with an unknown interviewer, London 1971*

When I started to compose, after the war, there were
many different directions in musical research which had
been prepared by the great masters Schoenberg, Webern,
Berg, Stravinsky, Bartók, Varèse. I had to go to the roots
of their individual work, and find an underlying unity. It
fell to me to synthesize all these different trends for the
second half of the century, perhaps in a similar way that
Heisenberg, in the first half of the century, had the role of
bringing together the discoveries of Planck and Einstein in
atomic physics.

My debut as a composer came in 1951. I was
twenty-three, studying music and piano and doing my

final exams at the state music conservatory in Cologne. At the end of my studies I wrote a piece called KREUZSPIEL, 'Cross-Play', which was performed in public at Darmstadt the following summer. I had composed other pieces but considered them simply stylistic exercises. We were given assignments to write a piece in baroque style, a fugue in Bach style, pieces for piano in Beethoven style, and I went further and composed a piece in Schoenberg style, which was not set by the professors, but just something I wanted to do. Another piece I wrote in Hindemith style. I never considered these as compositions: I was extremely conscious of the difference between imitation and originality, and much too intellectual to accept these plagiarisms of mine as original works, so studies in style they remained.

KREUZSPIEL did not just fall out of the sky. I was informed by a Belgian composer, Karel Goeyvaerts, about the work of Messiaen. There was a very special moment at this time when Messiaen's students — Boulez, Barraqué, Philippot, Michel Fano, Yvonne Loriod and Yvette Grimaux — persuaded him to synthesize the different influences that he had already incorporated in his own work; influences from the Viennese school, because they were more interested in them than in their own tradition of Debussy and Ravel, and the techniques of Indian *raga* and *tala* that Messiaen had learned from Indian music.

This led to the composition of a number of piano pieces, among them *Mode de valeurs et d'intensités* 'Mode of values and intensities', and *Ile de feu* 'Fire Island', in which, following Messiaen's researches in early renaissance music, we find duration formulae and pitch formulae treated with equal importance, and the length of silences having the same importance in the musical structure as the measured durations of the sounds. We also find influences of his researches in twentieth-century music, in particular the music of Anton von Webern, in which the motif and musical themes are ultimately reduced to formulae of two notes, so-called intervals.

From Goeyvaerts I learned about this synthesis process in Messiaen's music. He also introduced me to Webern's music, which I didn't know before because no scores or records were available. René Leibowitz was the only one in Paris who owned scores of the Viennese composers, and we all shared and made copies of Schoenberg, Berg and especially Webern, by hand. Goeyvaerts explained the technique of Webern for me, and analyzed his own piece, the *Sonata for two pianos*, which I did not understand at all. This was terribly exciting, to discover that there was music which I couldn't make sense of. Webern's two-note formulae were reduced even further, extending the idea of a melody of tone-colours, represented by different instruments, or vowels, to one of giving each note a different duration, a different dynamic, a different pitch, a different form of attack.

For all of us who were students of Messiaen during this time this was the point of departure: a music in which all the possible characteristics were differentiated from note to note. The description 'star music' was used casually by a music critic in Cologne, Herbert Eimert, after hearing these piano pieces of Messiaen, because the music sounded like stars in the firmament. The term 'punktuelle Musik' ('point music') was one I was using at the time.

At the 1951 Darmstadt summer school for new music

Goeyvaerts and I played his piano sonata. Only the middle movement: the two fast movements were too complicated for me to learn so quickly. We played it in public during the open seminar on composition, and it was violently attacked by Theodor Adorno. At the time Adorno was considered to be an authority on the avant-garde movement: he had just written *The Philosophy of the New Music* and in this book had literally destroyed Stravinsky as a reactionary, Schoenberg being the only name he would accept. Adorno was actually conducting the seminar in place of Schoenberg, who was very ill and died later in the year, and he attacked this music of Goeyvaerts, saying it was nonsense, it was only in a preliminary state, was not through-composed, but only a sketch for a piece that was still to be written.

The second movement of this *Sonata* was indeed 'point music': just isolated tones, though nowadays it sounds strangely melodic. Adorno couldn't understand it at all. He said, there is no motivic work. So I stood there on the stage in short pants, looking like a schoolboy, and defended this piece, because the Belgian couldn't speak German. I said, but Professor, you are looking for a chicken in an abstract painting. That's when I began to have my doubts about intellectuals and so-called specialists, even among the avant-garde. It showed that even though Adorno had been a student of Alban Berg and had composed a great deal, and though he wanted to be known as a composer more than as a philosopher, he was not basically a creative person. A creative person is always most excited when something happens that he cannot explain, something mysterious or miraculous. Then he is very nervous.

Now a lot could be said about relationships between our work and the Modulor of Le Corbusier, who tried to lay the foundation of a new method of architecture based on the blue and red series of proportional measures. The word 'series' in a context of structural design comes up again and again in architecture and other fields of constructivist art. We could speak of the strong influence on musicians during the early fifties, of certain books for the general reader by Einstein, or Heisenberg, of biologists like Weizsäcker, or Norbert Wiener.

There was similar thinking everywhere: reduction of the process of forming to the smallest possible element. When I use the word 'forming', I mean it in the sense of the crystallized result of the creative act, the form being just an instant in a process, and that what was happening among scientists as well as artists in the early fifties was that attention was increasingly focussing on the process.

According to Viktor von Weizsäcker, a German medical specialist and biologist, things are not in time, but time is in things (*Gestalt und Zeit*, Verlag Vandenhoek & Ruprecht, Göttingen, 1960). That is very important, in leading away from objective astronomical time to a consideration of organic, biological time. It was especially important for the musicians who started anew, after the war, working very systematically with individual notes. The evolution of electronic music did not happen by accident either, but literally as a result of discussions between Goeyvaerts and myself on achieving the objective of synthesizing even the individual notes, the timbre of the individual sound. The preformed nature of instrumental sounds — clarinet, piano, and so on — and of the way these sounds are produced, their physical limitations of breath, fingers and speed, were too restrictive for what we wanted to do. We wanted to achieve a unified musical structure, and therefore to make our own timbres, in order to find a coherent system to derive the macrostructure from the microstructure, and vice versa.

I use the words 'point', 'group', and 'mass' in order to generalize what is happening in music, and to make it clear that each is a particular manifestation of a larger trend. Point music flourished for only a relatively short period. We should have composed many more pieces and gone into point music more thoroughly; there is still a lot to be done in the future and opportunities to be much more daring than we were. I should like to see point music being composed in the future in which individual notes and sound events are spread out into a much larger timespan than we ever dared to do at the time. But then, people were absolutely shocked. They said, what do individual notes mean? And we were naturally somewhat influenced by this. Even I thought the distance between notes was enormous. A silence of two seconds was something I could barely accept myself: I felt it was too long, the next note should begin. Nowadays a silence of ten or twelve seconds is something most composers are terribly afraid of, because the audience would start talking and not listen to the music any more. So the longest silences I have used in my pieces are up to a minute in length (though in my theatre piece ORIGINALE of 1961 I did include a silence of two minutes.) A radio broadcast would be switched off if that happened, because the engineers are instructed that when a silence is longer than fifteen seconds they have to switch off because something is wrong with the equipment. We have certain conventions about sound and silence, and these conventions are only changed very slowly and gradually.

The drawback of point music is that if one wants the music to be different all the time, it becomes very monotonous because trying to be different from element to element becomes something they all have in common. I composed a work for orchestra in 1952, called PUNKTE 'Points', in which the relationship of notes and silences is not always clearly audible, because some notes are longer than others, or louder than others, and they overlap with shorter and softer notes, and mask them completely. And if you cannot hear the softer sound, you cannot say how soft it is, or how long, or where there is a silence. There is a problem of how to give the elements equal importance which people can hear. For example, I would have to make the softest elements very long, and the loudest elements very short.

After PUNKTE I composed KONTRA-PUNKTE 'Counter-Points'. The term has a completely new meaning, because it literally means point against point, not melody against melody, which is what counterpoint has meant since the fifteenth century, and which is associated with a particular sort of musical mind. The beginning of KONTRA-PUNKTE is point music, with a maximum of differentiation. That's natural, because I had to start the composition with pure point music in order to break away, so to speak, from my own system. As the work progresses, more and more small groups appear, that is, sequences of notes played by the same instrument, and eventually the piano comes to the fore playing a whole mass of notes.

The second stage of that process of musical thinking

that I'm trying to describe, brought the introduction of groups. It arose as a result of the composers having to be the teachers, and continuing to formulate a systematic approach to musical composition.

By group I mean the number of notes that can be separately distinguished at any one time, which is up to seven or eight. And they have to have at least one characteristic in common. A group with only one characteristic in common would have a fairly weak group character. It could be the timbre, it could be the dynamic: let's say for example you have a group of eight notes which are all different in duration, pitch and timbre, but they are all soft. That common characteristic makes them a group. Naturally, if all the characteristics are in common, if all of the notes are loud, high, all played with trumpets, all periodic, all in the same tempo, and all accented, then the group is extremely strong, because the individual character of each of the eight elements is lost.

So what is happening now is that more and more groups are combining with individual notes, and from that time on the point doesn't exist as a separate category any more, because it becomes one of the definitions of the group: if I have three notes, four notes, two notes, one note, five notes, six notes, then the one note is the smallest group. It's a question of context.

It might appear, from the way I am describing it, that I was following some divinely pre-ordained plan for twenty years. That was not the case: I did not talk in these terms at that time, it is only now that I can simplify things by classifying them in this way.

My composition GRUPPEN 'Groups', you may know is a work for three orchestras which surround the public in a horseshoe form. Each group of players has its own conductor, because they play in different tempi superimposed, which is impossible for one conductor and orchestra to realize. We say individual notes have their own durations; here, the important aspect is that the groups have their own modes of time, or tempi. That is something that has never occurred in Western music since the introduction of the common beat into music in order to control the vertical dimension of polyphony. In group compositions we come more and more to distinguish regions by their metronomical time, and I use chromatic scales of tempi corresponding to pitch, between MM=60 and MM=120, which is a ratio of 1:2, like an octave on the keyboard. Since then I've composed many times with chromatic tempi as composed with chromatic pitches.

The notion of group is transcended in GRUPPEN, just as in KONTRA-PUNKTE the notion of point was transcended by introducing groups. This is always happening, and is always very interesting. If one concentrates on something, or on a certain aspect, then one transcends it, because one cannot be content to remain permanently in a closed system.

What seems to be interesting in this context is this: whereas all music up to that historical moment, even the music of Webern, had been made by using certain *Gestalten* (figures), objects like a theme or a motif, and then transforming this object, varying it, transposing it, putting it into sequences, even destroying it or developing it further, in the music written since 1951 there was an explicit spirit of non-figurative composition. We tried to avoid all repetition of figures, and through this it became very clear to us that the way sounds were organized was the most important aspect, and not the particular *Gestalt* that occurred in a given moment.

The fact that certain notes were composed as points, and others as groups, that was what mattered: being recognizably points, or being groups, or a mixture of both. The groups could be completely different in their intervals or in their shape, and the points could be in different regions and of different overall quality, generally shorter or longer or higher or lower. I once made the comparison with sonata form, first-movement form in traditional music, where the best examples are the most through-composed, where the development is most advanced. As you know, the fifth symphony of Beethoven is always quoted as the example: there is just one figure which recurs all the time. As I say, always the same object in different lights. Whereas since 1950 it has been always new objects shown in the same light, and that light is, for example, a series of proportions.

There is a unity underlying all the different events which occur. That is why, when we listen to this music, we shouldn't become caught up too much with their differences, but try to sense and discover the underlying proportioning principle — the genetic principle — that gives birth to them all.

COMPOSING STATISTICALLY

From the lecture MUSICAL FORMING,
filmed by Allied Artists, London 1971

When we cannot count the individual notes in a group any
more, they surpass the group. If someone wants to join in
and play with our group, I say, well, fine — but five in a
group is good, six is already dangerous. And seven: with
seven the mass begins. Because then completely different
relationships among human beings begin to act. I said,
when we cannot count the elements any longer, so this
depends on the speed: naturally when the pace is too fast
we can't count them any more and thirteen notes may just
appear like a gesture, one doesn't feel like counting them.
Or there are too many events all happening at once, like a
swarm of bees; when you perceive the swarm as a shape, it
becomes a single entity. If we see a tree, we don't count the
leaves, but are still able to tell a pine tree from a beech. It

is an effect of the elements, but there is something else, the shape, the overall form, that characterizes the mass.

I still remember a moment during my musical education in the conservatory at Cologne when I was given a composition exercise. At the time I had no thought of ever becoming a composer. I showed it to my teacher: it was two measures of a great many notes in a small amount of time. And he said, who is going to hear that? Who can hear these notes? You don't control what you are writing. You see, what's the point in writing notes if people can't hear them? I said, oh well, I don't want you to count them. He said, well, what do you mean? Look at all these notes here. I said, I want this: frrp! He said, well just put one note; be precise, it's better.

So it was unthinkable. Some time later, in order to justify what I was interested in, I did an analysis of the music of Debussy which was later made into a radio broadcast, and the programme was subtitled 'Remarks on statistical form'. I was thinking about trends in registers of certain textures, about increasing and decreasing trends in density and in the character of density overall, of gradual shifts in predominating colours, from dark to bright, or from metallic to muted colours, and so on. This was a completely new language of musical analysis; I spoke of textures being perforated — I used the word textures as opposed to structures — and of rising or drifting shapes, sawtooth shapes of masses. It is easy to imagine, you can draw them.

When I was composing GRUPPEN for three orchestras, I had a little room in Switzerland for three months, and there was a small window in front of my desk through which I could see the incredible shapes of the mountains on the other side of the valley. There are quite a few groups in GRUPPEN which follow exactly the shape of these mountains: I became quite expert in drawing the outlines during that time. I would take such a shape and divide it vertically into musical measures of equal duration, fundamental durations, let's say they were whole-notes. Then I would add horizontal lines forming a grid, and subdivide each line going up from the fundamental into two, three, four units and so on, like overtones, but in the field of rhythm, until the shape was completely filled. So I was thinking in terms of shapes, of musical masses, and I could also make negative shapes, windows in these masses of sound.

In 1956 I realized the electronic work GESANG DER JÜNGLINGE 'Song of the Youths' in the studio for electronic music of West German Radio in Cologne. In this work it is possible to hear the realization of statistical processes. For example, I would give my three collaborators each a sheet of paper with a curve drawn on it, all of them to be executed in 20 seconds, to make a certain sound-event. And I would say to the first collaborator, this time start the pulse generator at 4 pulses per second, follow the curves of the drawing and end up with 16 pulses per second. To the second, who was working the potentiometer controlling the loudness level, I would say, let us take the dynamic range as being 40 decibels, from this maximum to this minimum, following the curve. To the third assistant who was in charge of the electronic filter, which lets through only a narrow band of frequencies from the signal, I would say, start at 3000 cycles per second, follow this curve for 20 seconds, and finish up at 400 cycles per second. We had a large stop-clock, we would start it, then on a count of three we would do the curves, and do them again several times until we agreed it was all right by everybody. After that, we would make seven more layers of 20 seconds, each one a little different, according to my definitions, and superimpose them all.

Naturally I can't say exactly at which moment a pulse will occur: all I can indicate is a general tendency during the curve. And the same is true for the dynamics and the filter. But if we superimpose a number of curves which share an overall characteristic tendency, then it leads to a certain result which is a mass: a mass moreover with a very distinct shape and a very precise tendency compared to another mass. This method of composition of musical microtextures by statistical methods has become very important in music. All the different applications of chance and random techniques in music are nothing more than derivations of it.

After finishing my music studies in the early fifties, I started again at the University of Bonn, studying communications science and phonetics. Simple analyses of noise sounds led us automatically to statistical wave structures. And the structures I found in individual sounds, like consonants, I expanded into a larger time-frame, deriving entire musical sections behaving in the same way as a single noise. I think that the most important innovations in musical form come about from building on the relationships of the three time regions: form, which is everything that happens between, say, eight seconds and half an hour; rhythm and metre, which is everything that happens between one-sixteenth of a second and eight seconds; and melody, which is everything that is organized between one-sixteenth and one-fourthousandth of a second, between 16 and 4000 cycles per second. It is almost technically possible to stretch a single sound lasting one second, to a length of half an hour, so that you have an overall form which has the characteristic structure of the original sound. On the other hand, if you are able to compress an entire Beethoven symphony into half a second, then you have a new sound, and its inner microstructure has been composed by Beethoven. Naturally it has a very particular quality compared to the sound resulting from the compression of another Beethoven symphony. Not to mention a Schoenberg symphony, because there are many more aperiodicities in Schoenberg: that would be more of a noise, whereas the Beethoven would be a vowel, because it is more periodic in its structure.

What I have said about point composition I would also say about composition in groups and in particular masses. We need to know better how to determine tendencies in masses of notes with greater precision. We have very little experience in this field; no research has been done in how a composer might continue in this field. I haven't done any systematic research, and research would be necessary from my point of view because in other fields I am working with very precise measurements. I simply have no precise knowledge of the behaviour of certain shapes in certain contexts; I just do it intuitively. And I don't deny that mistakes often occur: when I try to combine points with certain masses, and the points are completely masked, or when I think there is a difference between certain textures in a mass, and they don't come out in practice. I make mistakes in speed, where I think there are still differences recognizable at high speeds, and when it comes to the performance they are not, and I have to make changes in rehearsals. Finally, when I have to talk about these things to other composers, younger composers let's say, who want to work with me, then I find my language is not developed enough to speak about these things: I have to use mainly words from statistics and other fields.

We come now to the second set of terms, the terms determinate, variable and statistical. Points, groups, masses — all can be composed in any one of these ways. In most of my works I have composed points in a determinate way, or groups, or masses. What does that mean? It means that one can hear very clearly the intervals which make the proportions, the durations of the individual points, the shapes of the individual groups and masses. I don't really need to give examples of determinate structures of points, groups and masses because all of my scores, up to 1955, are completely notated in all characteristics in terms of regular scales and measurements. But a method of composing variable structures was a new phenomenon: what does it mean? I will give one example, and then leave it to you to invent more from your own imagination.

I composed a work ZEITMASZE 'Time Measures' for five woodwinds, in 1955, at the same time as I composed GESANG DER JÜNGLINGE. Five woodwinds: oboe, flute, cor anglais, clarinet, bassoon — is a traditional ensemble, but in this work you hear determinate structures alternating and mixed very clearly with variable structures. For example, there is a point where all five instruments start together. They have been playing chords. Everything organized in the vertical, such as chords, is clearly determinate because you would never find notes falling by accident together in a series of chords. It's an obvious sign of determination; even more so if there is a progression in a sequence of chords, from simple to more complicated and back, or as in classical harmony, from consonant to dissonant and back to consonant again. In this example, however, the starting-point is a point of departure where every instrument starts playing at a different speed.

So the oboe, for instance, is playing a given number of notes as fast as possible, the bassoon is playing as slow as possible, in an unrelated tempo; the English horn is playing an accelerando from as slow as possible to as fast as possible. (By 'as slow as possible' I mean for a woodwind player as long as possible to play a group of notes in a single breath. Actually that will vary with the size of the player's lungs, but that's not what I mean by variable: the timescale is clearly determined for any one player.) Another player starts as fast as possible and slows down in turn until he reaches a speed four times as slow. Then, after a longer time which is a time value within which everybody can finish playing their written notes, they wait for each other and come together again in the same metronomic tempo. This is easy to hear because the groups follow one another in a very precise manner, in sequence, or playing in chords, or in clear beats of three or four.

Sometimes one instrument is out of time with the others; there are sections where all five have individual tempos. There is a continuum between complete determination and extreme variability. And when we listen, we can feel when the music is very determinate because we know exactly where we are: on a certain beat, in a certain sequence of timbres, in a certain rhythm, but when we are in a region of high variability, the music is floating.

I said the word statistical is new in the context of music. Let me give an example from the seminar in communication sciences and phonetics which I studied with Professor Meyer-Eppler. This was a teacher who had come from physics and phonetics. In phonetics he was analyzing the different sounds of language, in communications science he was engaged in studying statistics, because he wanted to know more precisely what all the different noises were, and analyzing the wave structure of noises and consonants in language led him to use statistical methods of description and analysis. He would give us exercises demonstrating the principles of the Markoff series; in one we were given cut-outs of individual letters from newspaper articles, and we had to put them in sequence by a chance operation and see what sort of a text came out. Then we would repeat the operation with individual syllables, and then with combinations of two syllables, and so forth, each time trying to discover the degree of redundancy, as we called it, of the resulting texts.

Statistical means that you can permutate or change the order of events without it really making any difference, whereas if I were to change the order of the words and syllables I have just spoken, then there would be no direction or determination any more to what I am saying: it would just be an irregular distribution of phonemes. My composition ZYKLUS 'Cycle' is worked out according to different degrees of indeterminacy, with different degrees of statistical behaviour affecting certain groups of elements, groups or masses. That means the resulting music is constantly fluctuating between determinate and statistical behaviour. In ZEITMASZE, which is based on lines, it is possible to follow individual lines without difficulty because each is played by a different instrument and all you have to do is follow the colour of the instrument. In a statistical composition, however, the field becomes very much wider and it is not possible to follow precise lines.

In ZYKLUS I have worked with nine degrees of statistical distribution. I'm not saying that you are supposed to identify these nine degrees when you hear the music, nevertheless the music that results from such a method has very particular characteristics compared to other music, which is important in the context of this discussion. Statistical methods are introduced into musical composition in terms of bands and band-widths. By band I mean that every aspect is considered as occupying a position between a minimum and a maximum value: in pitch, a highest and a lowest pitch; in rhythm, a shortest and a longest duration; in timbre it may be between dark and bright. What is in between such limits is called a band and the band has a certain width. When the width of the band is zero, then we have a highly determinate situation: there is no choice. At the other extreme, when the band extends over the whole range of possibilities and I can choose, for example, any pitch, then the band-width is maximum. So between extreme determinacy and extreme relativity, indeterminacy, in a given composition, there is an entire range of degrees composed in terms of different band-widths. And some composers have become pretty specialized in statistical composition since these methods were introduced.

It happens every once in a while, in music as in other fields, that you find people specializing in one new aspect of musical forming, and becoming famous because they just specialize. A composer like Ligeti specialized for years in microstructures, the detailed composition of textures; or Xenakis, who has concentrated on stochastic distributions; or Penderecki, who was the cluster specialist for a long time. In another context we can see Feldman as being the specialist in music that is as slow, and as soft, as possible. Every once in a while music produces its specialists, people who go very deeply into their narrow specializations, and vary them all the time. This is something we take for granted in painting, more than in music. Everyone has his so-called personal style. By which is meant that he has narrowed down his field of activity so completely that it only takes a fragment of a work for you to say, ah, that's so and so.

And we can really say that universalists are becoming very rare in all fields, all the sciences. I tell my own students, if you want to become famous just take a magnifying glass and put it to one of my scores, and what you see there, just multiply that for five years. For example, if you see snare drums, then you start composing around twenty pieces only for snare drums. Snare drums of all different sizes: for fifty snare drums, for twenty, for thirty — snare drums on the roof, snare drums in the basement, big snare drums and very tiny snare drums, snare drums amplified and intermodulated. Then he will be the snare drum specialist, he will be known in Japan, he will be famous everywhere.

LYRIC AND DRAMATIC FORM

From the lecture MUSICAL FORMING,
filmed by Allied Artists, London 1971

We have traditional terms like theme, sequence and development, just a few musical terms, to describe the processes of classical music. And in the history of classical western music, development, as we find it in sonata first-movement form, plays an increasingly important role. At the same time as thematic development becomes more important, we find the number of themes becoming fewer and fewer, from three themes to two, sometimes even a single theme. Schoenberg's Third String Quartet takes this tendency to an extreme: as he said, 'everything is development'. Hauer was another Austrian with a similar idea: he said he wanted to construct a whole universe out of just a single mode. There was a general feeling at this time in history that scientists were very close to announcing the formula that was underlying the entire universe, the well-known *Einheitsformel* or unifying formula we often hear in connection with the name of Einstein. This simply says that everything is a development of one thing, which is exactly what Schoenberg says in that one composition: an initial theme, for example, or a series of pitches.

I have used the word 'dramatic' in talking about my earliest compositions. When we hear the word dramatic, we always think of it as meaning emotionally loaded. That's not necessarily true at all. Dramatic means to present figures, protagonists, as in Greek drama, and then develop to lead these figures to all different kinds of experiences. One gets killed, another one gets crowned king and a third goes mad. Still another one goes to America — not of course in the Greek drama, but that's the way things happen. Dramatic means that you can always follow the thread, even if you do lose it sometimes, which increases the dramatic tension. And music in the Europe of classical times had to represent the general interpretation of the universe. If the end was good, then everything was all for the good: so whatever happened in the meantime, there was always the recapitulation at the end to make everybody feel pleased and optimistic once more. In music this was certainly the case.

It all has to do with the classical concept of time. We find it in drama too, that convention of the forces for good eventually winning through. But there are many more dramatists, in England Shakespeare in particular, where the composition of the drama, as you know, is so constructed that it finishes by everybody being killed off; the conclusion was determined by the fact that they could not get out of the tomb and start all over again.

And we have quite a number of musical compositions which reflect this concept of how to interpret the evolution of the universe. It reflects the Jewish-Christian tradition in our culture, because how we interpret that beginning and that end has very much to do with our interpretation of the art of development. That particular initial moment and a very particular final moment; and then the drama so to speak in between.

My composition KREUZSPIEL is an example of dramatic form, but without that burden of traditional emotional expression. In my first compositions I had these ideas and they are beginning to reappear in my work nowadays. Development as a method of composing is governed by the arrow of time. If you listen carefully to the first movement of KREUZSPIEL, what you hear in the piano are six notes in the highest octave, and six notes in the lowest octave. During the movement, each note crosses over, one by one, passing through the seven octaves, until at the end of the movement the six notes that started in the highest octave are in the lowest, and vice versa. The development process can be clearly perceived because as each note crosses into the three middle octaves, it is picked up and played by two other instruments, bass clarinet and oboe. So the middle region gradually fills up towards the middle of the movement, and then empties again as the notes continue out to the edges. But it is a clear development, lasting all of two minutes.

This was my first work I considered to be a truly new composition, so to speak. However, I was still thinking in terms of *movements*, having composed student exercises influenced by Schoenberg, Beethoven, and so on, which were very dramatic in the other sense. So the second movement of KREUZSPIEL begins in the middle region and spreads out until it fills all the octaves. There is the same crossing of registers as before. Finally the third movement combines the tendencies of the two previous movements simultaneously.

In most of the music that has been composed since 1951 the idea of development has been abandoned, which to my mind is a shame. In the future I think we need more layers within compositions which have a strong directional orientation, and clearer developments. You know, there is a general tendency in literature as well to think that the thread of Ariadne, the idea that one should be able to follow the development of characters in a drama or a novel, is something very old-fashioned. Instead we find characters changing to such an extent that you don't recognize them as individuals any more; or people are introduced into a novel and then never appear again. Or on the stage, you now have someone playing a certain role, and then five minutes later there he is in a completely different role, then another, then another. So character development, continuity of the character, no longer seems to be important any more: what really matters is the way he appears, the manner of playing. Development should be re-introduced into musical composition, otherwise it becomes too weak, because too much importance is given to the individual event.

Another way of forming music is to work with sequences. Sequential and variation forms are based on a theme, which is not necessarily one you have written yourself: as we know, the greatest composers have composed large sets of variations on themes by other composers, or on folk tunes. You compose a sequence or a set of variations by adding them in series one to another.

The suite is a sequential form, nothing but a series of character pieces following one another like pop music performances today.

The more simple or primitive the music, the more you find sequence and variation forms expressing a need for change. Let's have a change: slow movement to fast movement to medium movement. A little sad, a little happy, a little aggressive, a little moody, and so on: the suite. Like the dance suite of the baroque, where it all began. We still find it in the classical symphony, a concert suite of four movements, one more dramatic, one more lyric, one more gay, one dance-like: rondo — which is another kind of dance form — with a recurring refrain after every derivation, then back to the same sequential formula at the end. Sequential forms: I call them epic forms because you can add to them and also play less, subtract, and it doesn't really change. Nevertheless, there were attempts, as early as Beethoven, to synthesize sequential and dramatic forms in one continuous development, like a long bridge. Beethoven was always dreaming of this synthesis of sonata form and variation form.

I can give an example of a more recent concept of sequential form, my composition MANTRA for two pianos and electronic modulation. In this work I use a 13-note formula, and nothing but this formula throughout the whole duration of the composition. The formula is expanded and compressed in its pitch and time intervals, but it is always the same formula. Each note of the original statement of the formula has certain characteristics: a periodic repetition, an accent at the end of the note, an ornament, and so on, and these characteristics are seeds of later development. The structure of the whole composition is an enlargement in time of that one small formula to more than 60 minutes, and the sections of the composition correspond to the notes of the original formula, and their characteristics. The form is sequential, but with an overall development.

Constantly renew and constantly repeat: that has always been at the heart of sequential form. In the beginning I and many other composers tried to avoid any form based on repetition or thematic development. Now, however, the formula is a means of re-introducing development to music, but in a completely new way. All the aspects of music that were taboo in the fifties and sixties are now returning again. I tried to avoid any recognizable rhythm; I banned periodicity, because it was too easy to grasp and remember, and dominated all the other aspects: my music was very aperiodic; I tried, like the painters in the abstract or informal period, to avoid any recognizable shape, any melody that you could whistle or sing, because it would take over your attention and you would always be listening to find out what was happening to it during the course of the music.

All recognizable sounds were avoided in electronic music: I used to say, don't imitate any traditional musical instrument, don't imitate a car sound or a bird, because then people start thinking of the bird and of the car rather than listening to the music. It was basically a weakness to have to demand a kind of exclusivity for each aspect of music, always to define music in terms of taboos. That's true in the arts as well as in life. It can be magical to discover something familiar in an unfamiliar setting, the more so when the context is completely abstract or informal. But there's always the question of whether it will come to dominate the piece. Whether you make use of quotation, or produce a recognizable sound object, if it is known there is a danger it will make everything else you have composed around it sound like a sauce, mere flavouring. One has to be very careful, introducing the banal into the unknown, because the known always tends to be the stronger and more inviting, like an old chair.

If I speak of a musical development as dramatic, when it is strongly directional, and epic, when it is sequential, then I could use the term lyric to describe a music in which the forming process is instantaneous. In my composition CARRÉ 'Square' for four choirs and orchestras, I tried for the first time to concentrate on instantaneous forming, or the forming of moments. It was, as many people wrote at the time, quite illogical, a complete reversal of normal musical convention. I worked on the basis of starting with the here and now, and then we will see if there is any past and future. This led to the approach I now call lyric, and in our western tradition the composition of lyric forms is very rare, given the predominance of sequential and developmental conventions. Not so in the oriental traditions, in Japan for instance, as we know lyric forms are much more frequent: the haiku verse form for example, and the conventions of the Noh drama and music. What counts there is the here and now; they do not always feel compelled to base their composition on contrast with what has gone before, or where a moment may be leading. You don't think about it: you are just aware of the counterpoint of foot, voice, hand, head, and eye.

And for long periods of time you have no thought for the

past or future, because there's nothing but the present moment. And if a sudden change occurs in the action, then it is frantically exciting, it is forming in that moment.

We have a few examples in the song repertoire as well, and perhaps the first beginnings of this concentration on the lyric aspect of forming are found in the music of Webern. The early pieces, the Op. 5 movements for string quartet, and even more so the Op. 7 Pieces for violin and piano, the Op. 9 Bagatelles for string quartet, or the Orchestral Pieces Op. 10, are so very short, we can call them moments, though they weren't called so at the time: the critics didn't know what to call them. It's music that is extremely condensed, pieces only twelve seconds, twenty seconds long. Just hanging in the air: nothing derived and nothing followed, that was it. Moments so very strong that Schoenberg could write of them — as he did in his Preface to the Bagatelles — that what others expressed in a novel, this composer could contain in an instant, a single sigh.

Extreme concentration. Well, I have developed the concept of instantaneous forming in my music, and now we can interpret it naturally as a development in terms of a particular organization of notes, and not as a fragment of a larger development. It's a different method; a different way of thinking, and it leads to different music.

You may realize that the great difficulty in moment-forming is the hair-raising problem of creating unity, because moment-forming is primarily about individuality. It has to be the degree of immediacy, or presence, that unites these individual moments: the fact that everything has presence to the same degree, because as soon as certain events are more present than others, then immediately we have a hierarchy: secondary events, transitions, accompaniments, preparatory events, echos, and that means direction and development of a sequential kind. And it is not at all easy to compose moments with equal degrees of presence.

It must now be clear that points can be determinate, variable, or statistical; groups can be determinate, variable or statistical; masses likewise can be determinate, variable or statistical. That points being determinate can be in a development, points being variable can also be in a development, and points being statistical can equally be in a development. That points being determinate can also be in sequence; points being in sequence can also be in moments; etc. This order of three times three terms: points, groups, masses; determinate, variable, statistical; sequential-forming, development-forming, moment-forming — is an order in which every term can be combined with every other term. And what this is ultimately leading to is not that one way of forming is avoiding other ways of organization, but can be combined with all the other methods. As I said, once we reach statistical ways of controlling it does not mean we forget about determinacy or directionality or variability, just as once we attain the lyric, we don't ignore the dramatic. Rather, what we are striving to reach is a universal conception, within which we may move in different directions from work to work and within individual works, but having all the possibilities of organization available to us in every composition.

Finally, why, you may ask, is it necessary to say all this? Why employ these nice terms in order to authenticate this wonderfully rich and unfathomable field of music?

Perhaps it is understood that these terms may apply to any music, folk music, or traditional music, or new music. What difference does it make? Well, for my part, I would like to say that I have experienced music in these terms myself, and my consciousness has been sharpened as a result. As consciousness is heightened, one's sensitivity is sharpened and that is what I am trying to do in explaining my way of approaching music, the music that I have composed, and that others have composed. To sharpen the consciousness, and with that become more sensitive.

MOMENT-FORMING AND MOMENTE

From the lecture MOMENT-FORMING AND INTEGRATION,
filmed by Allied Artists, London 1971

When certain characteristics remain constant for a while
— in musical terms, when sounds occupy a particular
region, a certain register, or stay within a particular
dynamic, or maintain a certain average speed — then a
moment is going on: these constant characteristics
determine the moment. It may be a limited number of
chords in the harmonic field, of intervals between pitches
in the melody domain, a limitation of durations in the
rhythmic structure, or of timbres in the instrumental
realization.

And when these characteristics all of a sudden change,
a new moment begins. If they change very slowly, the new

moment comes into existence while the present moment is still continuing. This meeting tonight is a moment determined by the measurements of the room, the number of participants, and to a certain extent the qualities of the people present. If you were to leave the hall, one by one, starting now, so that the last person left after about two hours, approximately when I am due to leave, then the change from this moment of the lecture to the next moment of going home or going elsewhere, will be a very slow process. On the other hand, if the floor gave way all of a sudden, or there were an explosion, the change from this moment to the next would be very abrupt.

The degree of change is a quality that can be composed as well as the characteristic of the music that is actually changing. I can compose with a series of degrees of change, or we can call them degrees of renewal. Then I can start with any musical material and follow the pattern of change, and see where it leads, from zero change to a defined maximum. That is what I understand by moment-forming. I form something in music which is as unique, as strong, as immediate and present as possible. Or I experience something. And then I can decide, as a composer or as the person who has this experience, how quickly and with how great a degree of change the next moment is going to occur.

MOMENTE ('Moments') is a composition which I started in January 1961; during the first week I designed and wrote all the sketches for the overall plan of the formal process. To those who know my previous works, it will be obvious that all the formal determinations did not simply fall out of the sky, but can be found in preparatory form here and there in earlier compositions. For example, the controlled randomness or mobility of the form as compared to one which is fixed and immobile. I will explain what that means.

There are three principal groups of 'moments' which characterize the work. The first group is the M-moments, in which melodic characteristics predominate; they are defined in the score by a capital M. The central M-moment is pure M, flanked on either side by moments M(d) and M(k), and each of them in turn gives rise to further combinations. They are the M-moments, the melodic moments, and they emphasize horizontality, heterophony. Heterophony is a way of articulating sound-events around a line, which can be a melody or just a glissando. It means that more than one source, let's say voices and instruments, are following the same line, but not all at the same time: not synchronized to the same beat, or clock, or other timing device. So what you hear is the result of several lines trying to go in parallel, but interfering with one another to produce something that is no longer a clear line but a heterophonic event.

Now suppose this is not happening simply by chance, but in a very controlled way, as for example in a lot of folk music. Then I could define how thick the line, the melody, may be at any given place; or I could go further and define an upper and lower limit within which the players are moving, so that this melody space will be more or less filled out. It's still a melody, but also heterophony: 'hetero' means many, 'phony' means sounding together. You find this a lot in Balinese music, for example, or in Vietnamese folk music.

Then there is a second group, called the K-moments, from the German word *Klang* meaning sound quality.

They are characterized by everything that functions as components of a complex sound, with vertical relationships: timbres, sound spectrums, chordal control, homophony. Homophonic music.

A third group is based on D: duration, *Dauer* in German. Moments based primarily on principles of measured durations, of different lengths, give rise to two important characteristics of any musical construction. One is silence; the other is polyphony, the superposition of more or less independent layers which are sounding at the same time. Let me explain. When I am working with a continuous melodic line of a particular shape, then the duration question does not arise. However, as soon as I start cutting the line into smaller sections, then I have to deal with different durations, and with the inevitable possibility that the fragments of melody may become separated, producing silence. Silence is the result of the concept of duration: to deal with durations means to break the flow of time, and that produces silence.

Secondly, once something is cut, the pieces can not only be separated but also superimposed, since they become independent of one another. And that superimposition produces polyphony. So the principle of polyphony and the principle of silence are both based on the concept of duration and the differentiation of durations; that is why I say polyphony is the most characteristic form of articulation of moments which are based on differences of duration.

Having distinguished the M, K and D characteristics as much as possible, by composing a purely melodic moment, a purely verticalized *Klangmoment*, and a purely durational, polyphonic moment, I am able to derive further moments from these centres which have elements more or less in common with the others. So there is an M(k) moment, which is an M-moment with a component of K: to be precise, about 30 per cent. The M(d) moment has a component of D characteristics. I can now build up a whole tree of different generations of inter-relating moments, and I can control very carefully how much they have in common. This is quite opposed to the traditional concept of building a musical continuum into which you then have to insert breaks, producing sudden changes, in order to sustain momentum. Instead of starting with something very homogeneous and then breaking the homogeneity, we start with completely separate instants: Now! Now! Now! Now! Now! — and then begin to determine how much memory or hope each Now may have — how much it may be related to what happened before or will happen next.

The mobility of MOMENTE, which I have referred to earlier, functions in the following way. The K-moments always remain in the centre of the work, when it is performed. But the conductor may decide on the order of the moments for a particular performance; they are all available as graphic material, written out in traditional and graphic notation, and most moments are contained each on one large page. The K-moments are always in the centre of the work, but the D- and M-moments on either side can be interchanged, giving either the D-moments at the beginning, then the K- and finally the M-moments, or the M-moments, then K-, ending with the D-moments. As for the large groups, so also for the moments within each group. At each branch there is a centre with two subgroups on either side, and each subgroup likewise is a centre with two subgroups; wherever there is a centre there is the possibility of exchanging the positions of the subgroups. It's like a mobile, and it means there is a large number of possibilities of combining these musical moments into a version fixed for a particular performance or series of performances.

Finally there are four I-moments: an I(m) with M characteristics, an I(d), and I(k), and a pure I-moment. The I means Informal, or extremely indeterminate, moments: fairly vague, static, without direction; they are actually the longest moments in the whole work, and they serve to neutralize the three main categories. I(m) and I(k) can switch places, but I(d) is always between them; the pure I-moment, however, always comes at the very end, and never changes position.

Now to the material. In all the M-moments the solo soprano predominates as the most linear sound-element in the entire composition, followed by the brass instruments, four trumpets and four trombones. Whenever the solo soprano is heard, the speaking voice and everything to do with speaking is especially prominent. From what I have already said about heterophony, it will be clear that there is also an emphasis on randomness within certain limits: of time, distribution of elements, of pitches, or timbres, of durations. Randomness is a particular characteristic of the M-moments; it follows that the central, pure M-moment, will be the moment whose elements are distributed with an extreme randomness.

The K-moments have a large choir of male voices featuring prominently, and in the pure K-moment there are only male voices. The characteristic instruments are the percussion: different groups of metallophones, a large tam-tam, cymbals — also the vibraphone, which is a metal percussion instrument of fixed pitches. Also skin instruments ranging from approximate to definite pitch, the latter with a special kidney-shaped drum I have discovered, which allows for the production of glissandi and a scale of precise pitches. In addition, a variety of percussion instruments that produce sounds like consonants: shhh, sss, rrr, etc. The sound of whispering, and noises resembling voiceless consonants, such as the sound of tube rattles, or the choirs shuffling their feet on the platform, everything of a noisy character and specific range, like fsss or fff, is given prominence, so whenever such sounds occur, you are aware that this is an influence of the K-moments, just as anything from normal to the most artificial kinds of speaking can be identified as an M-moment influence.

The third group, the D-moments, is characterized principally by female voices. They have to be clear as well as high in range, so that the melodic lines of the polyphony will be better distinguished in the higher register. Also electric organs, which allow durations to be precisely measured right to their very ends, without any decay of the sound, and then to be cut off sharply and clearly. Within limits this is also the case for the brass instruments and voices. So singing is the distinguishing feature of the D-moments. You can imagine how the combinations can be composed from the different ingredients: a moment D(m) as, let's say, singing with a little bit of whispering, or laughing, or sighing, or another element that comes from M. And those influences come in very precise doses.

With each moment there comes a certain number of

smaller score sheets having the same letter-name and an identifying number. These are called inserts, and each carries a characteristic excerpt from the moment itself. When the moments are arranged in a special order, there are instructions and arrows at the top of each moment which indicate where the inserts are to go. An arrow pointing to the next moment in a chosen sequence means to take an insert of that particular moment and putting it into the context of the next. There are slots in the score to receive inserts from previous or following moments, and the music which is inserted takes on certain characteristics of duration, speed, and dynamic curvature which belong to the host moment. At one extreme there are moments which give nothing and take nothing: they are neutral, examples of extreme self-containment. At the other extreme there are moments which take a great deal from their immediate environment, and give a great deal. Between these extremes there are many degrees of inter-relationship, which I have precisely determined.

The K-moments are all active. They influence others but are not influenced themselves. The strongest moment is the moment which takes the least and gives the least, and the weakest moment is the one you can hardly recognize for itself because it has so much in common with what has happened before and what is to follow. What I say about moments certainly applies elsewhere — to people too. Those who are so filled with memory and hope that they scarcely exist as individuals, or who are influenced by others to such an extent that you don't know them any longer, because you can't see them for reflections. Compared to them, the one who doesn't take anything, or need to take, but who influences others, is very strong.

What I have said about the internal structuring of MOMENTE also applies to the choice of material. I had certain material in mind while I was planning. I was thinking of a minimum of performers. A choir obviously, because I was wanting to integrate all aspects of language, a solo voice and groups of voices. Instruments, yes, I did think of using oboes for example, in combination with trumpets and other instruments, but forgot about them as the work progressed. In fact, the deeper I got into moment-forming, the less material I needed, because I was finding it more interesting to calculate very carefully how much and how little the moments would have in common.

The notation also reflects the internal relationships. What notation would you imagine for an extremely determinate D-moment, where you find an emphasis on polyphonic organization, rhythmic syncopations, etc.? Naturally classical notation is what you mostly find here. And in moments which have a large M-component of statistical randomness, we find graphic notation of fields within which the elements can be more or less freely distributed, and where the pitch is more indeterminate. For the choir I may simply give lines indicating the highest and lowest extremes of range, and indicate rising or falling inflections in between: so that is a relative notation of pitch. The same applies timewise: I draw a time box of a certain length, for a drum player, and the cue from the conductor is just a number 7, which means that during this timespan the player may perform seven strokes on drums — any drums. Or voices: I give them a list of seven nonsense syllables, or onomatopoeic syllables, written phonetically, like Oh! or Pooh! or Oi! or Ah! And every male singer in the group chooses a specified number to use as comments during a given number of seconds while the solo soprano is singing, whenever they feel like it. That leads to a controlled randomness of distribution of these syllables in time and naturally, order. And they listen to what the solo soprano is singing, or watch her, and say 'Oh-hh', or 'Wow!' or 'Oh-la-la!' — all of which are given by me in the score.

One of the possible beginnings of MOMENTE is the I(m) moment, an informal, indeterminate moment with M characteristics. I call it the applause moment. There is normally audience applause before the start of the performance, and if a version is chosen which starts with I(m), then the conductor comes on to the stage, makes his bow to the public, turns quickly around, gives a sign and the whole choir starts applauding the public. Then bit by bit, at signs from the conductor, this applause becomes gradually more structured. For example, all of a sudden it becomes rhythmical, then back to normal statistical applause; here and there the first syllables emerge from the bass singers, 'O that thou were my brother' (from the Song of Songs) — and then again, vertical blocks of applause. Then the trombones come in with clear pitches, so more and more this ordinary material is transformed into musical material, becomes musically organized.

That is one aspect of how sound material from everyday experience is integrated into this work; there is no clear dividing line between musical material and environmental sounds in this piece. Likewise for the choice of verbal material: in the K-moments particularly, I have used quite a lot of words and syllables, shouts that I have heard from the public during performances of my own music. Remarks like 'Stop it!', '*Bis!*', 'Ugly!', 'Beautiful!',

'Terrible!', or 'Be quiet!' — they are all incorporated, and I have indicated how these syllables should be delivered, sometimes strictly in rhythm, sometimes chanted in church style: 'Ug-ly, beau-ti-ful; ug-ly, beau-ti-ful'.

Then there is material that is a little more structured. At the end of this M(d) moment, for example, the solo soprano is given a series of syllables, like 'Me-me-me-me' and 'Nein-nein-nein' and so on, and she is asked to repeat them in any order, together with a number of intelligible words, and using this material to tell the choir singers a story. One day we were to give a performance at Donaueschingen, and on the day of the performance we were getting ready for the dress rehearsal when all of a sudden the orchestra assistant comes in and says, the trumpets and trombones have not arrived. So we had no trumpets and trombones during the dress rehearsal. The premiere was to take place at five o'clock in the afternoon; at 4.30 there were still no trumpets and trombones. There was great excitement, one and a half thousand people had arrived for this annual festival in Donaueschingen, a small village in the Black Forest in Germany. Then they decided on the spur of the moment to switch programmes with the LaSalle Quartet which was to play that evening, to give time for the trumpets and trombones to arrive by eight o'clock. I was in the hotel ready to go to the hall when someone said, no, no: you have to wait until tonight, we have changed the programme. About five minutes past five someone rushes into my room and says they have arrived, come, we have to perform. The trumpets and trombones were standing outside the hall warming up their instruments. They had come in a private car, and their part-books had simply been left behind at Cologne

Radio, and now there they were blowing into their instruments while the public was already waiting inside for the music to begin. I jumped on stage, said good luck to all of us, and we started.

Then, when the moment came for the solo soprano to begin her 'me-me-me' sequence — 'Impossible! — and the trumpets were not there!' And then, 'We were waiting all day, it's incredible!' to the choir singers, and one by one they began laughing. The whole moment became altogether real: 'Nein, but they didn't come, the trumpets, and we were waiting until *five past five*. Can you imagine this!' And they were burbling all this time and didn't quite understand, but the atmosphere became so heated up it was the most marvellous performance you could imagine.

There is text material that I found where I was working for a few months in an apartment in New York, at a time when I was teaching in Philadelphia, in books that had been left behind by the person who had lived there before me. In one book that I found there, *The Sexual Life of Savages*, written by a Russian scientist, Malinowski, I found many transcriptions of tribal rituals of the Upper Amazon and from South Pacific islands, and I have used quite a few as material. The one with laughter and giggling is an initiation rite for a young girl. I can tell you the meaning in private, if you like.

Other material is taken from letters from a friend: the whole work is dedicated to a young woman, is a composition that has to do with love relationships on many different levels. I took segments from her letters that used to arrive daily in the morning mail. 'Alles um mich herum ist nah und fern zugleich': that is one sentence, 'Everything surrounding me is near and far at once'.

There are many other sentences like this. In most moments there is material from the Song of Songs, a mythic love poem because we no longer know who wrote it, and most people know the text so you can assume that it is material that is immediately recognized, as well as being extremely beautiful. For the different moments I have been careful to choose excerpts which are more physical, less physical, or more on a spiritual level. 'O that thou were my brother', for example, has nothing to do with a sexual relationship when it first appears, so I use it sometimes in a very general sense of mutual affection.

The most lyric, the most subtle material, so to speak, was chosen from books I also did not have in mind when I started composing, but found in the same apartment in New York, in a book of collected poems of William Blake. There is one phrase which is heard very quickly, and later sung again very slowly and clearly by the solo soprano, undisturbed by anything else, which somehow expresses the essence of what I mean by moment, instant, now, here, the fulfilment, the degree of presence.

He who kisses the Joy as it flies
Lives in Eternity's Sunrise.

That's MOMENTE.

MICROPHONY

From the lecture MIKROPHONIE I,
filmed by Allied Artists, London 1971

For my work MOMENTE I bought a large tam-tam at a musical instrument fair in Frankfurt. The instrument is generally called a gong, but the correct name is tam-tam. This one has a diameter of about five feet, 155 cm. It can produce sounds which last longer than a minute from a single stroke. You have probably seen the monster tam-tam being hit at the beginning of the movies, followed by a lion opening his mouth and roaring. I have always associated the lion's roar with this tam-tam. The tam-tam didn't come from China in this case, but from Paiste, a family firm of father and two sons, originally from East Prussia and now based in Switzerland, also in North Germany. The father went to China and learned the technique of making these instruments there.

This tam-tam was hanging in my garden: I couldn't put it in the living room, it was too large. Every once in a while, when I went out for a walk in the garden, I would take a pen or a key, and scratch it, or just knock it with my finger, bang it with a pebble, write on it with the pebble, and then often lean my ear very close to the surface of the tam-tam, where I would hear all sorts of strange sound vibrations. At a distance of four or five inches away from the surface, these sounds were no longer audible.

One day I asked the technician, who used to work with me in the studio for electronic music at Cologne Radio, to come over to my house and bring along a filter. We have nice continuous filters in the studio which can be played like a musical instrument: they are bandpass filters which handle like a fader on a mixing desk, except they have two knobs moving independently or in parallel up and down, controlling the upper and lower limits of the frequency band-width. When you feed a sound through the filter, only the frequencies in between the two settings pass through.

I also asked him to bring a potentiometer, which is a device for controlling the level of a sound from a microphone. I had my own tape recorder set up in the living room. Then I took a basket, went into the kitchen and gathered together all sorts of implements — spoons, tumblers, rubber articles. I remember a clockwork eggtimer in a plastic case, wooden spoons and other wood objects, and several small plastic utensils. I walked to the tam-tam with that basket, took a microphone in my hand, wound the microphone cable round my arm to keep it out of the way, and then started taking the various articles one by one out of the basket and scratching, rubbing, every so often hitting them against the surface. At the same time I moved the microphone, mostly not in any premeditated way, just trying all sorts of movements in different directions: going away from where I was scratching, coming back very close, here and there, in all directions. And what I was doing and picking up with the microphone was being recorded in the living room fifteen yards away by the technician. At the same time he was also playing the filter, varying the band-width at random, and moving the potentiometer back and forth at random as well. He could not hear what I was doing fifteen yards away outside, so he was moving these controls completely in the dark. We recorded for about twenty minutes and then I walked in and said, let's hear it. And I must say that what we both heard was so astonishing that we started embracing each other and saying, this is unbelievable, a great discovery. We heard all sorts of animals that I had never heard before, and at the same time many sounds of a kind I couldn't have possibly imagined or discovered, not in the twelve years I had worked in the electronic music studio up to the time of that experiment.

On the basis of that experiment I composed the work which is called MIKROPHONIE I. 'Microphone' is in the title, signifying that the microphone is played as a musical instrument, and '-phony', as in symphony: microphony. I tried different numbers of performers at the beginning of work on the composition, then finally decided on two groups, each of three musicians. Let me describe what the three musicians in a group do. One is 'exciting' the tam-tam, as I call it: he uses all sorts of different implements to produce particular sounds, naturally having discussed with his fellow players which may be the best (I will tell you later how he knows what to look for). The second player in the group plays the microphone: he makes prescribed movements which are notated in a score. The third player of the group sits in the auditorium among the audience and operates the same kind of filter we used in the original experiment, and a potentiometer, and the output of these two devices is relayed to loudspeakers in the hall. We always use four speakers, in the corners of the hall, and the output on each side goes to a front speaker and a back speaker. What the audience hears is primarily what is coming from the loudspeakers; only occasionally are you able to hear the sound of the tam-tam itself, when it is played very hard, and the sound is very intense. Because there are two loudspeaker groups and two potentiometers per group, the sound can be made to move from front to back, as you can do with the balance control on a home stereophonic system. So naturally the musicians on the platform must also be able to hear the sound coming through the speakers, as well as the people in the hall.

And what they hear, in fact, is the result of two production lines, one in which the player who excites the tam-tam can hardly recognize what he is doing because the microphonist has already transformed the sounds he is making, and the filter/potentiometer player is doing something else again to transform what the first two are producing. So within each sound channel, every sound event that comes through the speakers is the outcome of a multiple interference of the actions of the three musicians in each group. Nobody can say what the sounds really are, other than tam-tam sounds: we cannot describe them purely on the basis of what we hear coming from the loudspeakers. (There is something very characteristic of our conventions of analysis — not only for new music, but in other areas too — that the further we go into the microcosm, the more we have to describe what we are observing in terms of the tools we are using.) So while we are getting more or less what our instruments can provide, there remains a lot of mystery about the sounds produced directly in the tam-tam itself. They are amplified, enormously amplified; they are filtered; the microphone is moved so the original waveform is continuously transformed. And all we know is what we get from a certain action. This is what I mean in general by microphony, the microphonic process. The microphone is no longer a passive tool for high fidelity reproduction: it becomes a musical instrument, influencing what it is recording.

The actions of each group are indicated in a score. The score is divided into three layers. The upper layer is for the exciter who plays on the surface of the tam-tam, the middle layer is for the microphonist, and the bottom layer is for the player of the filter and potentiometer. The tam-tam player's part is subdivided into three registers: high, middle and low, indicating relative pitch. The microphonists's part also subdivides into three, but indicating relative distance, moving across the tam-tam, from the point of excitation on the surface. Then for the filter player a similar subdivision of part into three indicates high, medium and low registers of filtering (actually the filter that we use has nine more or less equidistant frequency divisions between 30 and 12,000 cycles per second, so the player can work on a basis of three levels per register). All the time measurements are drawn to scale, with more precise indications for tempo and rhythm. The thickness of the notated lines for the tam-tam player indicates relative intensity: the thicker the line the more intensely you play.

For the microphonist the thickest line means closest to the surface of the tam-tam, the thinnest line the furthest away, moving perpendicular to the plane of the tam-tam. Now what does this produce? The closer the microphone is to the tam-tam, the more brilliant and direct the sound in the speakers; the further I move the microphone away from the tam-tam surface the more reverberation is mixed with the sound. It goes away in space, as though coming from the back of a large hall, and at the same time it is somehow muted in timbre. When I move the microphone across the surface of the tam-tam, however, the sound becomes softer and at the same time loses high frequencies. The colour of the sound changes as a result of being detected indirectly through the body of the instrument. So we always have this triangle of possibilities of microphone movement with respect to the point of excitation, affecting the dynamics, the timbre, the degree of reverberation of each sound.

The filter does the same. The higher the filter is open the brighter the sound: if the filter is only open in the middle and low regions, the sound appears darker. When the filter is completely open, then all the frequencies of the original signal can be heard. This affects the dynamics as well, since the more you reduce the band-width, the softer the sound becomes because the more energy from the original signal is rejected. Once again, all the characteristics of the sound are influenced by the player of the filter. He can superimpose a rhythm on what has already been produced by the other players; he can make the sound brighter, or louder, or softer. This is a very strange situation, having three players working on the same sound. And there is an inner polyphony within each sound, a superimposition of different rhythms and dynamic curves. This is something we haven't known before in music. Only very rarely do the players all work in parallel, in exactly the same rhythm, and with the same dynamic movements — let's say when the one plays louder the microphone simultaneously comes closer and the filter opens wider. Most of the time they do different things, the composition is polyphonic. And I can't predict what the result of this interference of the three players will sound like, because you don't know until you hear it.

Now we come to the question of how I describe these sounds which were so unfamiliar when I first heard them amplified and filtered. I first tried to describe the actions; in fact I initially worked out a score which gave instructions such as 'Take a plastic box of a particular size (I would give the exact size), and hold it against the surface of the tam-tam at a specific angle (and I tried to describe the angle), and then scratch it with a quick movement. . .' etc. This score became incredibly complicated in its description of the playing materials, and I felt it was absurd to have to write a score in 1964 saying this sort of thing. So I abandoned completely the description of the process in terms of measures and tools. I didn't even want to prescribe the materials any more: whether rubber, or wood, or metal or glass.

Then I said, what shall I do? How can I ever recover this sound world, even approximately, in any future? And how can this piece become a model for similar processes? What I did was the following: I made a scale. This scale went right back to the dawn of music, so to speak, to the kind of language the technician and I used when we were talking about the kinds of sounds we produced, and I would say things like, you know that sound there that went 'Rrrruf! Rrrruf!' and he'd say yes, I remember. You see, that's all we could do, and it is actually more precise than saying 'like a dog', because it was never exactly like a dog and it doesn't matter anyway. So I made a scale of 36 steps from the darkest and lowest sounds to the brightest and highest, and I used words to describe them. For example, 'wispern' in German: 'whisper'. I have been trying to find similar onomatopoeic words for sounds in English. 'Zischen' we say: I explained these words by describing actions, I said to my English friend how do you describe the sound when you open a bottle of mineral water? And he said ah, 'fizz'. And that was the sound I meant. So I made a list of words from the highest and brightest sounds to the darkest: rumbling, hooting, then there is a place where I have indicated tromboning, and they said that word doesn't exist in English, and I said well, if you have trumpeting why don't you have tromboning? They said well, okay, people will understand.

You have to be as precise as possible, and not give two or three words which might be mistaken for almost the same sound. For example, I have a sound which in German is called 'schwirrend', and they said, well, that's 'fluttering'. I said 'flutter'? That is not 'schwirren' like the wings of a bird. They said, it is 'fluttering' in English. I said, there must be a word with a higher vowel more like 'schwirrend'; in our language it's the same as the word for an arrow flying through the air. Ah, they said, you need 'whistling', but you must say it is an arrow otherwise it is the same as whistling a tune. Well, two words is okay, I can put 'whistling arrow'. So we have two English words, whistling and fluttering, for 'schwirrend' which is in my scale. Do I hear 'swishing'? 'whirring'? It's wonderful to try to bring order to these words: you should try it at home, it's very interesting to make a scale. Because once you have the scale then you have something that is certainly more precise than our traditional vocabulary for describing instrumental timbres in music, which simply identifies the object making the sound with the sound itself, as we say a tuba, or a flute, or an oboe, meaning the sounds they make.

That is the whole problem here, because we are trying to identify sounds directly, because we don't know the objects that might produce them. So we are looking for a language to describe sounds in themselves, and this kind of scale for sounds is badly needed. There is the so-called Oswald catalogue which is also quite a recent development, which gives a scale for all the perceivable colours; for many years now I have been working on the problem of a similar scale for sounds. There are suggestions to do it with numbers, and other suggestions to do it with words: I think ultimately it will be a mixture of technical description, in terms of frequency bands, attacks and decays, together with words.

Anyway, in MIKROPHONIE I all the structures I have composed have a word or a group of words to indicate the sound that the musicians should aim for. And they take this list of words and then they go shopping, that's what they did in Cologne, for tools to make whispering or fluttering sounds. And then they come back, for example with a plastic propellor fan of the kind you see on office desks, and plug it in, and the plastic blades start turning, and they hold it against the tam-tam, and it makes a sound that's pretty close. Someone else says, oh, wait, I will bring something else, and we try to get even closer to a characteristic fluttering sound, or whispering sound respectively. That's how we did it: for weeks meeting every day or every other day for several hours, trying out a lot of material on the tam-tam and deciding which would be the best.

In many cases we found better solutions by working together than the original suggestions I made from the experiment. We went to specialist shops where you can get, for example, all kinds of rubber: tubes, blocks, natural rubber, artificial rubber. And for some sounds we used them. Again, we tried all kinds of brushes on the surface, to get the shhh, ssss, thhh sounds. We tried rubbing sheets of architect's drawing paper together, to get the sound ffff, and then crumpling it, to make a crackling sound. For trumpeting and hooting sounds we took cardboard tubes of different sizes, and cut them to different lengths to make higher and lower sounds. The sound of snoring we got by using an open carton like a washing powder box, and pulling the edge down the surface. Chirping like crickets we got with a small plastic box, but for whispering we used the voice. For singing sounds, which are not vocal in this case, we made a monochord out of a piano string stretched very tight across two screws fixed in a piece of wood, and when you hold the string against the edge of the tam-tam and bow it with a cello bow, you can get a singing sound, and you can change the pitch by varying the length and pressure of the string, and make changes of dynamic while you are bowing.

For other sounds we used glasses. To make a high

singing sound like you get when you wet your finger and make a circular movement around the edge of a wine-glass, you have to put a little chalk or stringplayers' resin dissolved in turpentine on the surface of the tam-tam, otherwise there is not enough resistance when you draw the glass down the surface. That is one possible interpretation of singing sound. I like the fact that there are several possibilities for each word, but the characteristic quality in relation to other sounds is always preserved.

I should say that in addition to this score, which is fairly abstract in that it leaves to the discretion of the performers what materials they use to produce the sounds corresponding to the instructions, I have also prepared a realization score for publication, as a safety measure. I have learned over the years that it is better to give a written example than leave matters completely in the open, because as you know, tapes of performances get lost and eventually deteriorate; and I want this work to develop and to be performed in the future. It is interesting to imagine this score being discovered in say five hundred years, when maybe even plastics have disappeared and God knows what kind of beings will be on this earth. It would be quite funny from the future point of view, to see how we interpreted the score. So there are photographs of all the implements we have used, and it really looks like a table full of garbage: it's unbelievable. The old cardboard and rubber articles are mostly showing signs of wear from many performances; the glasses are half broken; there are wine bottles and all sorts of other things. It looks very strange. And I photographed each article, numbered the photographs and numbered the corresponding words in the score, and I have written a detailed commentary indicating how each one was used.

What we are actually doing is listening to a tam-tam, an instrument of a kind over three thousand years old, like a doctor with a stethoscope listening to the body of a person. This has many implications for the future. Quite a few composers have since applied microphones to actors, singers and instrumentalists in a similar way; the microphone is now accepted as a musical instrument since MIKROPHONIE I. Someone said, must it be a tam-tam? I said no, I can imagine the score being used to examine an old Volkswagen musically, to go inside the old thing and bang it and scratch it and do all sorts of things to it, and play MIKROPHONIE I, using the microphone. Play anything. Discover the micro-world of the acoustic vibrations, amplify it and transform it electronically. That's why I call it 'electronic live music' as opposed to electronic music which is produced in a studio.

FOUR CRITERIA OF ELECTRONIC MUSIC

From the lecture FOUR CRITERIA OF ELECTRONIC MUSIC
filmed by Allied Artists, London 1971

Four criteria of electronic music. The first criterion is the unified time structuring. The second criterion is the splitting of the sound. The third, the multi-layered spatial composition. The fourth, the equality of sound and noise — or better, of tone and noise.

New means change the method; new methods change the experience, and new experiences change man. Whenever we hear sounds we are changed: we are no longer the same after hearing certain sounds, and this is the more the case when we hear organized sounds, sounds organized by another human being: music.

Until around 1950 the idea of music as sound was largely ignored. That composing with sounds could also involve the composition of sounds themselves, was no longer self-evident. It was revived as a result, we might say, of a historical development. The Viennese School of Schoenberg, Berg and Webern had reduced their musical themes and motifs to entities of only two sounds, to intervals. Webern in particular, Anton von Webern. And when I started to compose music, I was certainly a child of the first half of the century, continuing and expanding what the composers of the first half had prepared. It took a little leap forward to reach the idea of composing, or synthesizing, the individual sound.

I should say immediately that it was a second thought, because I started first of all by analyzing all sorts of sounds. I was twenty-three and working at the *musique concrète* studios in Paris. I recorded sounds in the Musée de l'Homme, where you can find exotic instruments of all kinds: instruments of wood, of stone, of metal; instruments of different cultures and historical periods. I also analyzed sounds and noises which I recorded from daily life, and began to study books in which you can find spectral analyses of the sounds of classical musical instruments. Bit by bit, not having had any proper training in acoustics at the music conservatory or at university, I became aware that sound is more than just an experience. I became very interested in the differences between sounds: what is the difference between a piano sound and a vowel aaah and the sound of the wind — shhh or whsss. It was after analyzing a lot of sounds that this second thought came up (it was always implied): if I can analyze sounds which exist already and I have recorded, why can I not try to synthesize sound in order to find new sounds, if possible.

At that time the only instruments available which tried to imitate classical instruments were those you found in nightclubs, not in the symphony orchestra, which even now is still a fairly closed sound world because of its social composition. You won't find, for example, electric organs of the modern type in the normal lineup of a symphony orchestra. On the other hand, pop music makes use of a range of specially manufactured keyboard instruments with registers to imitate trumpets, flutes, clarinets and so forth. Today all sorts of gimmicks have been added to transform these sounds; then there were fewer gimmicks, nevertheless there was a certain variety of synthetic timbres which the composer might choose, like a painter choosing colours to mix from. Classical orchestration is traditionally an art of mixing.

To synthesize a sound you have to start with something more basic, more simple, than the sounds you encounter in daily life. I started looking in acoustic laboratories for sources of the simplest forms of sound wave, for example sine wave generators, which are used for measurement. And I started very primitively to synthesize individual sounds by superimposing sine waves in harmonic spectra, in order to make sounds like vowels, aaah, oooh, eeeh etc., then gradually I found how to use white noise generators and electric filters to produce coloured noise, like consonants: ssss, sssh, ffffh, etc. And when I pulsed them it sounded like water dripping.

From these primitive beginnings I began, as many others were then doing in the *musique concrète* studios, to transform recorded sounds with electric devices. For example, to speed up sounds: everybody who has a record player knows how to speed the music up or down just by changing from 33 to 45 or vice versa. Well, we have been able since the late forties to change the speed of a tape recorder continuously, not just in steps, and so to transform sounds by speeding them up or down. This is very important. Let's immediately jump to the extreme, and then we come to the first criterion.

1 THE UNIFIED TIME STRUCTURING

Suppose you take a recording of a Beethoven symphony on tape and speed it up, but in such a way that you do not at the same time transpose the pitch. And you speed it up until it lasts just one second. Then you get a sound that has a particular colour or timbre, a particular shape or dynamic evolution, and an inner life which is what Beethoven has composed, highly compressed in time. And it is a very characteristic sound, compared let's say to a piece of Gagaku music from Japan if it were similarly compressed. On the other hand, if we were to take any given sound and stretch it out in time to such an extent that it lasted twenty minutes instead of one second, then what we have is a musical piece whose large-scale form in time is the expansion of the micro-acoustic time-structure of the original sound.

I started to compose sounds in a new way around 1956. I recorded individual pulses from an impulse generator, and spliced them together in a particular rhythm. Then I made a tape loop of this rhythm, let's say it is tac-tac, tac, a very simple rhythm — and then I speed it up, tarac-tac, tarac-tac, tarac-tac, tarac-tac, and so on. After a while the rhythm becomes continuous, and when I speed it up still more, you begin to hear a low tone rising in pitch. That means this little period tarac-tac, tarac-tac, which lasted about a second, is now lasting less than one-sixteenth of a second, because a frequency of around 16 cycles per second is the lower limit of the perception of pitch, and a sound vibrating at 16 cycles per second corresponds to a very low fundamental pitch on the organ. The timbre of this sound is also an effect of the original rhythm being tarac-tac rather than, say, tacato-tarot, tacato-tarot, which would give a different tone colour. You don't actually hear the rhythm any more, only a specific timbre, a spectrum, which is determined by the composition of its components.

Now imagine speeding up the original one-second rhythm one thousand times, so that each cycle now lasts one-thousandth of a second: that will give you a sound in the middle range of audibility, of a constant pitch about two octaves above middle C on the piano. A frequency of 1000 cycles per second, and a particular timbre. I made a lot of experiments with different rhythms in order to see what they would give as differences in timbre. What we perceive as rhythm from a certain perspective, is perceived at a faster time of perception as pitch, with its melodic implications. You can build melodies by changing the basic periodicity, making it faster or slower for the sound to go up or down in pitch respectively. Within the basic period which determines the fundamental pitch, there are what I call the partials, which are subdivisions of the basic periodicity, and they are represented here by the inner divisions making up the original rhythm. These are perceived as the timbre.

If I change the periodicity of the sound: a little faster, a little slower, or to be more precise, make the duration of each period a little shorter or a little longer, then the sound starts oscillating around a certain middle frequency, and all the half vowel or half consonant components, which are already fairly broad-band, begin to break up. So the continuum between sound of fixed pitch and noise is nothing more than that between a more and a less stable periodicity: the noisiest noise being the most aperiodic. This discovery of a continuum between sound and noise, the fourth criterion of electronic music, was extremely important, because once such a continuum becomes available, you can control it, you can compose it, you can organize it.

If now we slow down the speed of a given rhythm we come into the realm of form. What is form in music? Well, we usually say a musical structure of between the one or two minutes of a piece of entertainment music, and the hour and a half of a Mahler symphony, which is about the longest we encounter in music of the western tradition. (There are a few operas from the end of the nineteenth century which last longer, and which introduced some very important expansions of musical time, but there is nothing in our tradition like the Omizutori ceremony of Japan, in the Temple of Nara, which lasts three days and three nights without any break, or like certain tribal rituals still to be found in Ceylon or parts of Africa.) So, according to the fixed perspective of our tradition form varies between dimensions of around one minute and ninety minutes. This corresponds to 1, 2, 4, 8, 16, 32, 64, 128 — a range of around seven octaves. Amazingly enough, we find a similar seven-octave range within the traditional formal subdivisions of music, from the length of a phrase, the smallest formal subdivision, say eight seconds, to the largest complete section, or 'movement', of about sixteen to seventeen minutes' duration (8 – 16 – 32 – 64 – 128 – 256 – 512 – 1024 seconds). So there is a range of about seven octaves for durations from eight seconds up to seventeen minutes. Between eight and sixteen seconds, durations become less and less easy to remember. It has something to do with our perception: if I ask you to compare a duration of 13 seconds with one of 15 seconds, you hardly know the difference. If I ask you to compare a sound of one second with a sound of three seconds' duration, on the other hand, the same difference of two seconds appears enormous. Our perceptions are logarithmic, not arithmetic, and that is important. Rhythm has its own field of perception and between eight and sixteen seconds there is a transition between our perceptions of rhythm and form.

Rhythm and metre are organized in measures, traditionally to a fixed periodicity or tempo for a given movement, say fast, or medium fast, or slow, because everything was based on dancing or body actions, and that's where the music came from. A periodicity of eight seconds is perceived as very slow: we are already entering the region where form begins. Subdivide eight seconds, and you have 8, 4, 2, 1, a half, a fourth, one-eighth, one-sixteenth. One-eighth, eight attacks per second, is about the fastest we can play with our fingers: it is a limit determined by our muscles and bodily construction. I could go faster perhaps, to twelve or fourteen, by rolling my hands in a special way, but no more. There again, you see, the range is seven octaves $(8 – 4 – 2 – 1 – \frac{1}{2} – \frac{1}{4} – \frac{1}{8} – \frac{1}{16})$: it's very interesting.

With sixteen attacks per second, we reach what we call pitch; between eight and sixteen, there is another transitional region where it is difficult to know what the sound really is. And as we know from the keyboard of the piano, there are seven and a half octaves in the range of fundamental pitches: from 16 to around 4000 cycles per second. Above that we perceive only brilliance.

The ranges of perception are ranges of time, and the time is subdivided by us, by the construction of our bodies and by our organs of perception. And since these modern means have become available, to change the time of perception continuously, from one range to another, from a rhythm into a pitch, or a tone or noise into a formal structure, the composer can now work within a unified time domain. And that completely changes the traditional concept of how to compose and think music, because previously they were all in separate boxes: harmony and melody in one box, rhythm and metre in another, then periods, phrasing, larger formal entities in another, while in the timbre field we had only names of instruments, no unity of reference at all. (I sometimes think we are fortunate in having such a poor language to describe sounds, much poorer than the visual field. That's why, in the visual field, almost all perception has been rationalized and no longer has any magic.)

There is a very crucial moment in my composition KONTAKTE for electronic sounds, beginning just before 17' 0,5" in the printed score. A translation of the title might be 'Contacts', and the contacts are also between different forms and speeds in different layers. The moment begins with a tone of about 169 cycles per second, approximately F below middle C. Many of the various sounds in KONTAKTE have been composed by determining specific rhythms and speeding them up several hundred or a thousand times or more, thereby obtaining distinctive timbres. What is interesting about this moment is that if I were to play little bits of the passage one after another, like notes on the piano, nobody would be able to hear the transition that takes place from one field of time perception to another. The fact that I make the transition continuously makes us conscious of it, and this effort of consciousness changes our whole attitude towards our acoustic environment. Every sound becomes a very mysterious thing, it has its own time.

There is a very important observation which was made not so long ago by Viktor von Weizsäcker, a German biologist who started in medicine, which says that the traditional concept is that things are in time, whereas the new concept is that time is in the things. This is quite different from the traditional concept of an objective, astronomical time represented by our clock, which measures everything according to the same units, and is the same time for everything. Instead, the new concept tells me as a musician that every sound has its own time, as every day has its own time. This is new in musical composition, to think in terms of an individual time-event, which then takes its own time to be put together with other sounds.

The end of the transition in KONTAKTE which I started to describe is a sustained note, E below middle C, which when I reached it I worked on for another four minutes, making very small changes in pitch. Other sounds pass by, as if you are looking out of the window of a space vehicle, but the line of orientation remains. You hear it go right away into the distance, then come back.

2 THE SPLITTING OF THE SOUND

The same sound serves for another section of the composition KONTAKTE, beginning approximately twenty-two minutes into the tape, which I use to clarify what I call the splitting of the sound. If we understand that sounds can be composed, literally put together, not only stationary sounds which don't change, but also a sound like owww, which changes in the course of its duration; if we can compose these sounds, in the sense of the Latin *componere* meaning put together, then naturally we can also think in terms — note the quotation marks — of the 'decomposition' of a sound. That means we split the sound, and this can be much more revealing in a certain context than hearing a unified sound on its own terms, and comparing it to another which is happening at the same time or immediately before or after it.

You hear this sound gradually revealing itself to be made up of a number of components which one by one, very slowly leave the original frequency and glissando up and down: the order is down, up, down, up, up, down. The original sound is literally taken apart into its six components, and each component in turn is decomposing before our ears, into its individual rhythm of pulses. In the background one component of the original sound continues to the end of the section. And whenever a component leaves the original pitch, naturally the timbre of the sound changes.

So what has this got to do with composing? What makes this more than just an example from a lecture by an acoustician or a physicist who says: 'Today I am speaking about the subject of sound decomposition and this is what it sounds like'. If it were no more than that, music would be reduced to a teaching aid — and the previous example too. This is the point: whereas it is true that traditionally in music, and in art in general, the context, the ideas or themes, were more or less descriptive, either psychologically descriptive of inter-human relationships, or descriptive of certain phenomena in the world, we now have a situation where the composition or decomposition of a sound, or the passing of a sound through several time layers, may be the theme itself, granted that by theme we mean the behaviour or life of the sound. And we live through exactly the same transformation that the sound is going through. The sound splits into six, and if we want to follow all six, we have to become polyphonic, multilayered beings. Or when the sound falls six and a half octaves, you have to go with it, because if you stay put in your time chair, as it were, you won't perceive it. That's why many people get a strange feeling in the pit of the stomach when they hear the sound falling down. So there you have it: the theme of the music, of KONTAKTE itself, is the revealing of such processes, and their composition.

Of course it could be done more or less intelligently. I mean, a physics professor would just have gone straight down six and a half octaves, and leave it at that. Someone else might just, well, vary it a little, make it a bit more inventive. If the same process is composed by different people and one is more imaginative than the other, then that's all there is to say, about the process, and about the difference between a physics professor and a composer in this context.

There are many visual artists today who are mainly concerned with the exploration of new ways of seeing. Seeing itself is the theme: how to look at things and what we can see, the widening of our perception. Having said that, I must say that most examples of this kind of art that I see in galleries are absolutely vacuous: one look and that's it, you've got it. Or it makes your eyes flicker and you say well, okay, looking at such things makes your eyes flicker. One begins to feel like those animals in experiments which have to respond in a certain way to a particular stimulus. Much of modern art is like that. We are in a very important transition from the traditional way of perceiving art to a new way of making and perceiving art, and discovering new functions for art, that it is revelatory. It reveals our existence and ourselves, and thereby changes us as human beings.

This change in perception will bring about incomparable changes in humanity in the next hundred years, spiritual and physiological. Don't imagine we remain the same when our perception is changing so drastically, now that our musical perspectives have become relative instead of absolute. Take timing: when I have to pass quickly through the continuum of speeds and tempi in music, I change completely, and am no longer comparable to someone who is fixed in his time perspective of metronome 70, his heartbeat, or metronome 20 or 30, his breathing, for whom everything that is faster is fast, and everything that is slower, slow. What we need, and what we will become as individuals — some of us — are beings who are able to change their speed and direction of response very quickly, experience all these transformations, and yes, become the sounds.

As I say, people in general occupy a certain middle position in time, from which they judge what is fast and what slow, and this middle position is determined basically by the body, by the breathing, the heartbeat, the speed with which the limbs — including the fingers — can be moved, the tongue, lips, head and so on. All these limits determine a middle range of speed, and everything that is faster or slower we judge from this standpoint. The same is true for the voice, which has a natural middle register, and which for most people is fixed, from which we judge sounds to be higher or lower. It's very hard, in a musical composition of a more modern character, to move the listeners out of their middle region into another, let's say into a very fast region, for long enough for the fast to become normal and everything that was medium before to appear slow. Or the other way around, to slow an audience down with music like Japanese Gagaku music, which is very much slower than traditional western music, so that having listened for a long time to this very slow music, everything medium in speed is perceived as fast.

That will give you an idea of the change of perspective which has come about from the enormous expansion of musical timing. Nowadays a modern composition switches very fast from one time layer, one tempo, to another, whereas, as I said before, in traditional music we find a slow movement, a fast movement, with a break in between, then a minuet movement, then a very fast movement, staying at a particular perspective long enough in each case for the listener to feel safe. Naturally, with the arrival of modern transport, our context of experience has changed a lot: in everyday life we can experience many different time perspectives. If I am driving in a car, and I see someone walking past, and there is an airplane passing overhead, the airplane can be very slow compared to the person walking; or if I am overtaken by a train, that can be extremely slow compared to a cyclist coming from the opposite direction. If on the other hand I leave my car and go on an airplane, in my experience I am exchanging a very fast time for a slow time, because compared to being in a car, where the trees go by very fast, the experience of being in an airplane is very slow.

So in real life we may change time very quickly, and modern man has to change his time perspective just as quickly, and if he doesn't he gets sick, or even dies, because the degree of change is just too much. The same applies to space. Musical space has been fixed in the western tradition, for as long as musicians gave up running through the woods for sitting on chairs on a stage. The function of space has been neutralized in our western music. Some conductors, for the sake of instrumental effect, make changes in the positions of players in an orchestra, for instance putting the celli at the left side instead of the right, but such changes have no real revealing function: it's still fixed, it doesn't move, all it serves to clarify is the music being a static object in space. It has something to do, I should add, with the fact that until very recently it has not been important to be able clearly to identify sounds which come from behind, say 270°, like a ship's navigator, on a circle of 360°, or one which comes from say north 15° with 45° of elevation, or south 170° from an angle of minus 40° or 50°. In the concert hall we always have the same perspective, the one seat as a point of reference, which is determined, or has been up to now, by how much we can pay.

Well, I discussed at length with my studio technicians about 1953, whether it would be wise to put musicians in chairs and swing them around, for example, and many said they might object. So then we thought it would perhaps be preferable to let them play into microphones and connect the microphones to speakers and then swing the speakers around, and then they would not object, but they objected to that too. They said, oh no, you can't do that with me: I'm here, and the sound has to come from here. Well, we are not birds, that is the problem. If we were birds, then naturally we would not argue that way, but we are clumsy and would rather sit in one spot — in fact, most of the audience can't even stand, let alone move during a concert, so our perspective of musical space is utterly frozen. And it has led to a music in which the movement and direction of sound in space has no function.

But the moment we have the means to move sound with any given speed in a given auditorium, or even in a given space outdoors, there is no longer any reason for a fixed spatial perspective for music. In fact, that is the end of it, with the introduction of relativity into the composition of movement and speed of sound in space, as well as of the other parameters of music. And this movement in space of music becomes as important as the composition of its melodic lines, meaning changes in pitch, and as its rhythmic characteristics, meaning changes in durations. If I have a sound of constant spectrum, and the sound moves in a curve, then the movement gives the sound a particular character compared to another sound which moves just in a straight line. Whether a sound moves clockwise or counter-clockwise, is at the left back or at the front, or alternating between left back and right front, or any other combination, these are all configurations in space which are as meaningful as intervals in melody or harmony. So from the time these means of moving sound have been available, I have been speaking of and composing and finding a notation for space melodies, to indicate movement up or down in space, or describe a particular configuration in a given space, at a certain speed.

The culmination of this concept came about, happily thanks to a lot of diplomacy, at the 1970 World Fair in Osaka in Japan. I was given the chance to realize, in collaboration with an architect, a project I had first described in 1956. It was a spherical hall seating six hundred people on a platform in the middle, which is sound-transparent. They entered by a moving staircase and sat down wherever they wished. There were cushions: the Japanese like these. The platform was a metal grid, and there were speakers all around: seven circles from bottom to top, three below and four above the platform, arranged in ten vertical rows around the audience. A sound source, a singer, player or tape recording, could be sent to any point in this pattern of speakers. Singers and soloists worked from six crow's nest balconies around and above the central platform; their sound was picked up by microphones and sent to a mixing desk where I or one of my assistants would be sitting. I had two soundmills constructed, each having one input and ten outputs, allowing a chosen sound to be rotated by hand at speeds up to about five revolutions per second, in any direction. For example, I could decide to make a voice go in an upward spiral movement for two or three minutes, either clockwise or anticlockwise, while at the same time another player's sound moved in a circle using the other soundmill, and a third crossed in a straight line, using just two potentiometers. So we were able to realize a free spatial composition. It could be improvised or predetermined, but we had a wonderful time improvising for six and a half hours every day for 183 days. It was wonderful playing with these things.

And the Japanese would come in and sit. They are very polite. Then I would start: the house lights would go out. It was very beautiful: wherever there was a speaker you could see a pattern of five little lights. It looked like a night sky, a very geometrically composed sky of stars. I would sit down; then the players would appear, I would introduce the players in English, it would be translated by a hostess into Japanese, Mr So-and-so will now play a duo with Mrs So-and-so — and then we'd start. I could always see the hall from the control desk. These were mostly simple people, many with babies on their backs, and at the first sound everyone would look round in astonishment, and try to follow it with their eyes. And after a session of fifteen to twenty minutes they would walk out turning their heads like geese and making spiralling movements with pointing fingers. So even if they had never heard new music before, it was still exotic stuff, as their music is exotic stuff to us. Nevertheless, new music or old music is of little importance: what is important is that they went out imitating the movements they had heard, and I was very happy. If you discover something really new, which affects human experience, I mean, there's no discussion, that's just the way it is. All the rest is minor talk about little details. But that was important, it was a new experience.

It was a wonderful building: they destroyed it

afterwards. I tried to get it to Europe, it was not very expensive, I must say. It was a geodesic construction with a plastic skin, very well made. And it worked acoustically: everyone said a sphere never works well, you get sounds bouncing up and down, but the sound was wonderful, very good acoustics and good reverberation. One day I will get it back. Certainly it was such an important experience for the first time in history to have the sound moving in a controlled way around the listener, with the listener at the centre. If you don't have good auditoriums, the way I recommend to hear music where the movement of sound is very important, is with earphones. That way the sound moves within you and your head becomes this sphere, and with a little imagination you can expand this sphere to any size.

3 THE MULTI-LAYERED SPATIAL COMPOSITION

Multi-layered spatial composition means the following: that not only does the sound move around the listener at a constant distance, but it can also move as far away as we can imagine, and also come extremely close. These characteristics are distinctly different, so I'm being cautious when I say that I have managed to superimpose acoustically only six layers up to now, and that it is very difficult to add more layers. At the end of the section in KONTAKTE where the sound is split into its separate components, about twenty-four minutes into the tape, there are dense, noisy sounds in the forefront, covering the whole range of audibility. Nothing can pierce this wall of sound, so to speak. Then all of a sudden, at 24′ 18,7″ in the score, I stop the sound and you hear a second layer of sound behind it. You realize it was already there but you couldn't hear it. I cut it again, like with a knife, and you hear another layer behind that one, then again. Building spatial depth by superimposition of layers enables us to compose perspectives in sound from close up to far away, analogous to the way we compose layers of melody and harmony in the two-dimensional plane of traditional music. This is really very important, and nothing new in human experience: I mean, it happens everywhere. It's important to be able to hear whether the car coming towards me is still far away or not, because if I hear it's just two feet away, I will behave differently. Well, some people may think it doesn't matter in music, but beware: if the sound comes very close it can have the same impact on our own audioelectrical system.

Why should spatial perspective be typical only of electronic music? Have we not already encountered it in a Mahler symphony where the composer says that trumpets should sound outside the hall? Naturally we have, but such examples are fairly primitive: there is more to spatial perspective than playing loud and soft, with or without reverberation. Imagine, for example, that someone is whispering very softly in your ear, while a thunderstorm or a rocket taking off is going on ten miles away. You are still aware that the whisper is very soft, but it's close, whereas the rocket is very loud, but very far away. Now two things are necessary for hearing spatial perspectives: one, that we know what it is we are hearing, and two, that we know whether it is far away or close. When we have never heard a particular sound before, we don't always know whether it is far or close. We have to have heard it several times before in the context of the music, in order to know how it sounds when closer and further away.

There is something very important now to be said about our concept of perception. Our concept of perception dates back, as we all know, to Gutenberg: since printing we have become verticalized, and our perceptions have become dominated by the visual. Our conception of truth of perception is entirely built on the visual. It has led to the incredible situation where nobody believes somebody else if he can't see what it is. In every field of social life you find this need to establish everything in visual terms, because what you cannot see people do not believe. And this leads to the very strange response of most people listening to this music, that when they hear the sounds in a given hall are moving very far away, and coming very close, they say well, that's an illusion.

We now have the means technically to make the sound appear as if it were far away: 'as if', they say. A sound that is coming from far away is broken up and reflected by the leaves of the trees, by the walls and other surfaces, and reaches my ear only indirectly. There is a factor of distortion and noise. Naturally we are able to reproduce these noise factors synthetically. On the other hand, a sound that is very close to my ear reaches my ear directly, without reflections, and the unreflected sound can also be produced artificially. Whether a sound appears 'as if' far away or very close, depends on a combination of intensity and degree of distortion. The purer the sound, the closer it is, and in an absolute sense the louder it is.

Now I come to my point: when they hear the layers revealed, one behind the other, in this new music, most listeners cannot even perceive it because they say, well, the walls have not moved, so it is an illusion. I say to them, the fact that you say the walls have not moved is an illusion, because you have clearly heard that the sounds went away, very far, and that is the truth. Whether the walls have moved at all has nothing to do with this perception, but with believing in what we hear as absolutely as we formerly believed in what we see or saw. They open their eyes and they say, well now, aha, there are the walls, so that was an illusion, the sound has not really moved away. What makes it so difficult for new music to be really appreciated is this mental block in people, which makes them say 'as if', or that they can't even perceive what they hear. To hear a sound three miles away, they expect a person, a bird or a car to be three miles away: they identify the sound with an object that must be at the given distance. That's what we are struggling with, and that's what will change mankind as gradually more and more people perceive this music in its real terms.

4 THE EQUALITY OF TONE AND NOISE

The equality of tones and noises has already been made clear in discussing the continuous transition from periodic to more or less aperiodic waveforms. If the degree of aperiodicity of any given sound can be controlled, and controlled in a particular way, then any constant sound can be transformed into a noise. A noise is determined, as we say, by a certain band-width, or band of frequencies, the widest band-width covering the whole audible range (though to spread a sound to that extent one needs to repeat the process several times). In addition, there is the distribution of energy to be considered. The band-width might be the same for several noises, but their energy distribution might be quite different. Nowadays we have various electronic filters and modulators available to transform a steady sound into one that is more aleatoric in its inner structure.

As it has become possible to define a continuum between sounds and noises, completely new problems have come up for when we compose or play intuitively, because we have no training whatsoever in balancing tones and noises. Traditionally in western music noises have been taboo, and there are precise reasons for this. It began from the time when staff notation was introduced, and music could be notated in precise intervals for the first time. Then it was mainly vocal music, sung predominantly with vowels rather than consonants. If I sing a melody of consonants now, people would say it isn't music: we have no tradition of music composed in these sounds, and no notation for it. There you see how narrow our concept of music is, from having excluded consonants, then noises. Of course you find consonants in vocal music, but only in order to make a word comprehensible: that's the function of consonants in our daily language, to clarify meaning. But in a musical sense consonants have no function, other than as accents: ss or t or p or k to start or end a sound clearly.

The integration of noises of all kinds has only come about since the middle of this century, and I must say, mainly through the discovery of new methods of composing the continuum between tones and noises. Nowadays any noise is musical material, and it is possible to select a scale of degrees from sound to noise for a given composition, or choose an arbitrary scale, from the complete range. The balance between tones and noises is not at all a numerical one. When I was working on the final section of KONTAKTE, I wanted a situation where tones and noises were in balance. I wanted to deal with the whole scale of timbres between aleatoric and periodic, and I could certainly not use as many noises as tones, because noises tend to cover the tones, being so to speak more primitive. So, to establish a proper balance between the two in a given section of music one has to be careful to reduce the number of noises extremely in relation to the number of tones.

From this we discover more new principles of musical articulation, for example that I worked with forty-two different scales in this particular work. If you know the piano has a half-tone scale, twelve steps to the octave, then imagine forty-two different scales, where the octave is divided into thirteen, fifteen, seventeen, twenty-three steps, and so on. I have used a scale of scales, where the ratio of increase in the step size is constant from one scale to the next, and each particular scale is strictly associated with a particular family of tones and noises. Put at its simplest, the noisier the sound, the larger the interval, the bigger the step size. The noisiest sounds in KONTAKTE are two octaves in width, and the scale for these noises is the largest and most simple scale in the whole work: a scale of perfect fifths. A step size of a fifth means that twelve steps covers the whole audible range. The narrower the band-width, on the other hand, and the more the sound approached a pure tone, the finer the scale: this is the principle I have applied. With the purest tones you can make the most subtle melodic gestures, much, much more refined than what the textbooks say is the smallest interval we can hear, namely the Pythagorean comma 80: 81. That's not true at all. If I use sine waves, and make little glissandi instead of stepwise changes, then I can really feel that little change, going far beyond what people say about Chinese music, or in textbooks of physics or perception.

But it all depends on the tone: you cannot just use any tone in any interval relationship. We have discovered a new law of relationship between the nature of the sound and the scale on which it may be composed. Harmony and melody are no longer abstract systems to be filled with any given sounds we may choose as material. There is a very subtle relationship nowadays between form and material. I would even go so far as to say that form and material have to be considered as one and the same. I think it is perhaps the most important fact to come out in the twentieth century, that in several fields material and form are no longer regarded as separate, in the sense that I take this material and I put it into that form. Rather, a given material determines its own best form according to its inner nature. The old dialectic based on the antinomy — or dichotomy — of form and matter has really vanished since we have begun to produce electronic music, and have come to understand the nature and relativity of sound.

INTUITIVE MUSIC

From the lecture INTUITIVE MUSIC,
filmed by Allied Artists, London 1971

The term intuitive music is one I have purposely
introduced. Not only in order to make it clear that I have
something specific in mind, but also to rule out other
things. For example, music played freely without a score is
sometimes called free improvisation, like let's say free
jazz, though making free jazz has its own rules: as the
word says, it should still sound like jazz, otherwise people
would just call it free music. Then there is improvisation
in folk music, in India for example. But there is very little
actual freedom in this music. The system is very
restricted: an Indian musician learns from his master all
the rules of how to make small variations of the ragas
and talas, and there is very little personal invention,
practically none. This method of improvising has

changed very little in the history of music. I try to avoid the word improvisation because it always means there are certain rules: of style, of rhythm, of harmony, of melody, of the order of sections, and so on.

After 1964 I started to tour intensively with a group of players. I had done tours before, but then we played music that was determinate, precisely written in traditional notation. Now I became more and more daring in what I was giving my co-players and myself as graphic material. There was the score of PROZESSION 'Procession' which consists only of plus and minus and equal signs, and instructs the players to 'use events from my previous compositions' as raw material. The pianist draws on the Piano Pieces I–XI; the tam-tam player draws on events from MIKROPHONIE I: the viola player takes material from GESANG DER JÜNGLINGE and MOMENTE; the electronium player draws on SOLO, GESANG DER JÜNG-LINGE and I think also from MOMENTE. So each player takes his raw material from these previous works, and then transforms it according to transformation signs. All I have composed in PROZESSION are transformation signs, which tell what to do with the events they have chosen.

A plus sign means to play an event that is higher, or longer, or louder, or which has more limbs than the event you have just played, or that you have heard being played just before. A minus sign means play an event that is lower, or softer, or shorter, or has fewer limbs. By limbs I mean clearly-defined segments or components within a certain duration. If there is one limb, you hear only one attack, there is no segmentation. If I play ta-ta: finish, then I have two segments, or limbs as we say, *Glieder* in German. When the number of limbs increases, then it means a plus sign; with a minus sign the number decreases.

These four categories are always considered from one musical event to the next. Higher or longer or louder or more segments; minus sign, lower or softer or fewer segments or shorter. Equal sign, play the same as what you have just heard before or played yourself. That's all: a series of signs. The four players should play for any length of time greater than twenty-three minutes, I say in the introduction to the score. That is a duration we have found as a result of many performances to be the minimum required in order for the piece to develop. After that, the piece can end at any moment that a player feels it should end. The score also says that if you start a new performance and it sounds like the previous one, stop and start again. Likewise, if it comes to an end and the ending sounds like a previous ending, the players should continue and try to find an ending that has not occurred before.

You see, the process of transformation is emphasized more than usual, but what is transformed is less specific. What is given is genetic rules for the development of a music. The process goes further in KURZWELLEN 'Short Waves'. Then in 1968 all of a sudden I reached the moment in my composing where I gave practically nothing to the performer, even to myself as one of the players of our group. Then and there I wrote fifteen texts. In 1969 we recorded twelve of them over eight days, two hours per day, without prior rehearsal and in most cases without prior discussion. There were some we discussed, but they were texts we had played before in public.

The first text from this collection AUS DEN SIEBEN TAGEN 'From the seven days' reads as follows:

for circa 4 players

Circa already: four, maybe three, maybe five. But not seven.

RIGHT DURATIONS

Play a sound
Play it for so long
until you feel
that you should stop

Again play a sound
Play it for so long
until you feel
that you should stop

And so on

Stop
when you feel
that you should stop

But whether you play or stop:
Keep listening to the others

At best
play when people are listening

Do not rehearse

That's what we used, and there came out of it a performance of, I would say, half an hour, I don't remember exactly. This performance is on a record.

The next text has a little drawing at the top, a curve that goes up out of the paper and then comes back. It reads:

For ensemble
UNLIMITED

Play a sound
with the certainty
that you have an infinite amount of time and space

We played it for a whole night once, in St Paul de Vence, in the South of France, for a music festival. We started playing in a courtyard before the public arrived, then after about two and a half hours the musicians left, one by one, still playing and disappeared into the forest, from time to time coming back into the courtyard and disappearing again, until it all ended at about three o'clock in the morning.

Later I wrote commentaries on these texts. I said imagine someone having the certainty that he has an infinite amount of time and space. I haven't met any person up to now who has really and totally achieved that state; well, I mean, anyone can approach it. It leads to the most incredible sounds and musical actions, if you really think you have an infinite amount of time and space. You don't need to think when it is finished, or whether anybody is listening or not: you don't care whether you die in the meantime, or if the sound may be too long for you to finish playing, or if the space you need is greater than the hall, or your instrument, or your own body can contain. You have an infinite amount of space. That's it. When one really meditates on this text, it leads to the most incredible actions and sounds.

Another one is 'Connections', for ensemble:

CONNECTIONS

Play a vibration in the rhythm of your body
                                    (Of *your* body. The player's.)
Play a vibration in the rhythm of your heart
                                    (That's possible.)
Play a vibration in the rhythm of your breathing
Play a vibration in the rhythm of your thinking
Play a vibration in the rhythm of your intuition
Play a vibration in the rhythm of your enlightenment
Play a vibration in the rhythm of the universe

Mix these vibrations freely

Leave enough silence between them

Now, you can imagine what kind of reaction I got to these texts. From my co-players, who thought I had flipped out completely (I had, for some time, I must say, but in a very unusual way, not with drugs or anything) — not to mention the people who were not performers themselves, and who had no idea what such a stimulus can generate in a musical mind, well, in a musician. I'll give just a few comments. 'Play a vibration in the rhythm of your thinking.' When I gave a seminar that same year, 1968, in the Darmstadt International Courses for Contemporary Music, none of the fourteen young composers knew what I could mean by that. I said, just take a pencil, and every time your thinking changes direction, tap it on the table. We could do this together now; it would be quite interesting. These chairs are plastic, just take a pencil or a ring and just tap. The best way is to close your eyes, if not, you look around, and whenever you feel your thinking is changing, then knock on the chair . . . Could you try to slow it down please? Try to keep on the same thought, or block it out, stop thinking for a moment. You think, I am knocking, he is knocking, I am in the hall, oh my hair, how do I look? — each time tock, tick, tock. Slow it down, try to slow it down.

What I mean is, when this is done with musicians, then you will hear that every action has a reaction, a particular sound has many reactions, and you get groups of attacks, I mean, of changes, which happen very quickly. As soon as someone does something which attracts the attention, he interrupts someone who is trying to keep the same thought going, breaks the rhythm of his thinking.

Another example: it says here 'Play a vibration in the rhythm of the universe'. We have a pianist in our group, Mr Kontarsky, who is an extreme intellectual and everything must be intellectually and mentally clear, otherwise, he says, he at least can't do anything. So he said, what do you mean by the rhythm of the universe? What is all that mystic stuff here? And I said, I mean, have you never had dreams where you fly from star to star? He said, no, I don't have them. What are you talking about? Then I said, well, have you any inner view or inner vision of how the planets are rotating round the sun? — What do you mean? I said, at least you have an intellectual knowledge of how long it takes for the moon to go around the earth, or the earth round the sun; how many days it takes, in earth days, and how many earth days Mercury takes? And he said, I am not so well informed about the planets and, well, I could have thought about it but it's all so slow. I said, no, when it is in your mind it has your own time, hasn't it? Imagine it, just the rhythm of the universe. I mean, I'm not asking you tonight to go beyond the solar system, but just try. And he was saying, I don't know, let's stop and you can get somebody else. I said, well Aloys, you see, perhaps the constellations, think Cassiopeia or the other constellations of the stars. He said, Oh, you mean Webern? I said Yes! He said, well okay, let's start.

Well, the fact that some of you laugh shows that you share that understanding of Webern. Webern is the extreme constructivist of music: he worked with intervals and points which form very particular constellations. So from that moment, in this particular piece, this pianist has played what I call the bones, the most constructive elements, very few and far between, and all the other players attach themselves like flies on to the clear constructions he plays. Immediately he could do something with 'the rhythm of the universe'. I made a few suggestions and it clicked in his mind. But I have to say, when he came to the sentence 'Play a vibration in the rhythm of your enlightenment', then he simply had a long silence. Well, he was being very honest with himself and he said, I don't know what to do with that indication. When that indication comes I just stop and start again when the next one comes. That's fine.

Now I come to the text which is at the extreme, and which has brought more accusations against me as a composer than anything else during my whole life. Not only the music critics, but intellectuals in general were thinking that I had become a dangerous influence. The text reads:

For ensemble

IT

(IT is the title)

Think NOTHING
Wait until it is absolutely still within you
When you have attained this
begin to play

As soon as you start to think, stop
and try to re-attain
the state of NON-THINKING
Then continue playing

— and so on.

When we first played this text with our group, at a music festival in Brussels, we purposely had not played it before, and against all expectations, it worked.

Since that time we have never had any trouble. IT has been played by many other groups, and I have compared numbers of different performances of the same texts, and have found that they often share very similar characteristics. All the different versions of IT have started with very brief, short, sound actions; then gradually you get here and there a longer sound, which stops as soon as another sound starts, which shows that sounds are cutting off each other. Later in all the versions there is a gradual superimposition of sustained sounds: you have one musician playing, then another starts playing a sound or a certain pattern, and the first is able to keep going. Then it builds very quickly, in every version I have heard: all of a sudden there is a situation reached where they are obviously taken all together by something that is in the air, and are completely absorbed by the sound and react instantly, without thinking. I mean, they just do it, and then very dense structures come about. These last for some time, until at some point one of the musicians plays a sound that goes out of context; then abruptly there are long silences. After that, they try to recapture what they were doing before, but it doesn't work any more.

Of course sometimes you get rubbish. The first sign of it is when preformed material appears, citations, when you are reminded of something that you already know. Then we feel it's going wrong, that instead of automatically recording, there is something in us automatically playing back recorded rubbish. So then we stop. When I hear the Globokar group, for example, even though they claim to play without any written understanding or agreement, it is very obvious that the percussion player every once in a while starts playing tabla rhythms from Indian music. He studied tabla once with an Indian percussion player and these stylistic elements come out automatically. So while there may be no pre-established style for the whole music, certain stylistic elements come into it, and I would try to avoid them, and draw completely on intuition. The same is true for Portal, the clarinet player. Whenever the groups comes into rage, as I call it, when their playing becomes very heated, he starts playing typical free jazz melodies and configurations that he has played for years, being a free jazz player: certain idioms that come from the group he plays free jazz with, others that belong to the free jazz tradition in general.

Playing intuitive music it soon becomes very obvious which musician has most self-control; in fact, it's alarming how quickly the musicians reveal their physical and spiritual state, whether they are in crisis or have reached a certain kind of equilibrium. Musicians are easily carried away by not listening, and this is often the reason for a performance turning into rubbish, in the sense that they start to play very loudly, so loud that nobody else can be heard, and they don't realize what they are doing. Such players can become very totalitarian in certain situations, and that creates awful situations for the group playing together. Also their sounds become very aggressive and destructive, and at a very basic level of communication and production of sounds, destructive elements begin to work.

Understand, I am not talking about ugly or beautiful sounds, but about very debased, physical, bodily aggression expressed in a determination to destroy one another. Then they play all at once. When that threatens it is most important that I always remind them, and myself as well, 'Don't play all the time, and don't get carried away'. After several hundred years of being forced to play only what has been prescribed for them by others, musicians today are particularly apt, once they start playing intuitively in a group, to play all the time, and it becomes loud very soon, and they don't know how to get soft again because everybody wants to be heard.

The best number is four or five players. Even with five, it takes a lot of self-discipline to keep quiet for quite long periods during a performance, so that solos, duos and trios occur, and not only quintets all the time. And if musicians are dependent on technique, and they play in a technically self-conscious way, the intuition can't work well: they always want more than they can do, then it becomes rubbish again. That has been my experience. The best intuitive musician is really at one with his instrument, and knows where to touch and what to do in order to make it resonate so that the inner vibrations that occur in the player can immediately be expressed as material vibrations in the body of the instrument.

So finally there remains only one question: either all five players, me included, were liars or were cheating ourselves, or something was going on that worked. That leaves the objection of the intellectuals; well, they fool themselves, what do they mean? As someone who at different times in his life has gone deeper than most into his whole being and the structure of his personality, what the brain is, and what the mind is, when I say, I am thinking — who is saying this? Then this person who is saying, I am thinking, can just as easily say, I have decided not to think now. One is not identified with the brain, but with the brain activity, and that activity, the thinking activity, is something that is responsible to a higher self, one which uses the brain as a computer. That is all. So acting, or listening, or doing something without thinking, is the state of pure intuitive activity, not requiring to use the brain as a control.

You can think about a lot of things while performing: training your fingers, controlling what you are doing, reacting — aha! now he is playing, now I should do this — all of which is thinking about what you are doing. But you can also act: Now! Now! Now! Now! Now! Stop the thinking, and as soon as you stop, all right. As soon as reflection or thinking starts, also noticing that you are thinking, stop. That is all that is asked. And it needs some time for preparation, some special training of the musicians. I come back to the pianist: he said, it's impossible, I think all the time. What you are asking is absolutely impossible. Well, I said, can't you stop? He said, no, no, I can't stop thinking, that's ridiculous. When I am not playing I am thinking of my next concert or rehearsing the *Piano Piece X* in my memory. I am always thinking. I said, stop it. He said, how? And this was quite unusual for me because, I mean, these are the simplest things in life. When someone says, I can't sleep, and you say, well, stop thinking, then you will fall asleep right away. Or you just decide to sleep, stop thinking and then you can sleep at any moment. Most people can't do that. They haven't even thought about not thinking.

Well, it may seem funny, but it's deadly serious, and the musicians who work with me and who perform these texts quite regularly, at least they think about the possibility of what this might mean for them, and how they could practise it. I am trying to find a technique for myself as a composer and interpreter, and for other musicians who work with me, to extend the moment of intuition consciously, so that when I want to, it starts, and I am no longer helpless until it arrives, usually at the wrong moment, when I have no time or there is someone wanting to talk to me. And those moments of intuitive working must last as long as I want, but then I will have to find a completely new technique of making music. I can't sit at a table with a pencil and rubber, sharpen the pencil and write down what's coming from intuition, because intuition has a very particular kind of speed, which is by no means congruent with the speed of writing.

There are certain abilities required now in order to play this sort of music that I call intuitive music, that the traditional musician has never learned. He doesn't even have a thought about it. The most profound moments in musical interpretation and composition are those which are not the result of mental processes, are not derived from what we already know, nor are they simply deducible from what has happened in the past. Musicians must learn to become the opposite of egocentric; otherwise you only play yourself, and the self is nothing but a big bag full of stored information. Such people are closed systems. But when you become like what I call a radio receiver, you are no longer satisfied with expressing yourself, you are not interested in yourself at all. There is nothing really to express. Then you will be amazed at what happens to you, when this state is achieved; when you become aware of what happens through you, even for short moments, you will be quite astonished. You become a medium.

PART 2

SOME QUESTIONS AND ANSWERS

*The following interview with
Karlheinz Stockhausen
by Robin Maconie was recorded at the composer's home
in Kürten, near Cologne, on August 4 and August 7, 1981*

RM: Your more recent music makes a virtue of procedures we associate with the Synthi 100, and in particular the sequencer. For example, the expanding pitch-scales in MANTRA, *the sliding scales of tempi in* JUBILÄUM *'Jubilee', and the construction and transformations of melodies in* SIRIUS. *How important a role has the Synthi 100 played in your work?*

KS: The general view that pre-existing conditions — psychological, sociological, technical or otherwise —

explain artistic innovation, is wrong insofar as my work is concerned. I made known as far back as 1954 in lectures, and in 1955 in the article '. . . how time passes. . .' that I would very much like to have instruments which would allow the contraction and expansion of scales, not only of frequency, but also of durations and dynamics. I explained that I wanted scales of dynamic degrees to be as precise as scales of frequencies. It was quite a long time before people in the field of technical production of musical instruments heard of these new demands. I met several of them, and one, Zinovieff, told me that his designs of voltage-controlled instruments had been influenced mainly by my articles about my electronic music, and my scores, like ELEKTRONISCHE STUDIE II 1953–54 'Electronic Study II', which is based on a very special scale of the 25th root of 5, GESANG DER JÜNGLINGE, and KONTAKTE, the pitches of which are organized in forty-two different scales.

The Synthi 100 was bought for our electronic studio in Cologne Radio at the beginning of the seventies. I visited Zinovieff in London several times to discuss the requirements of expansion and contraction of scales of tempi, of melodies in their interval construction, and naturally of durations. I required extremes of expansion and compression, at least 1000 : 1, which the Synthi 100 could not satisfy; Zinovieff said he would work on it, and I later heard an example of a new instrument with further possibilities, but it did not go into production. So the synthesizer I used for SIRIUS, and the one which proved that my dreams could be realized, at least in part, was the Synthi 100: it is still the instrument I like best, because it allows the speeds and registers of *all* parameters to be manipulated *in real time*, through keyboards and joysticks and a lot of buttons.

This ability to influence every parameter at the time of listening is an essential requirement for electronic music in the future. And also for instrumental composition: for example, I am now working on LUZIFERS TRAUM 'Lucifer's Dream' for piano and bass voice, the first scene from SAMSTAG AUS LICHT 'Saturday from Light'. And I am constantly aware that I am working in five time-layers which stem from the superformula for the opera for seven days of the week, LICHT. SAMSTAG is one 'limb' of this superformula, as I call it, and one small section of this limb is the nucleus of the first scene. Three of the five time-layers come from the superformula, the other two belong to the scene. Each layer runs at a different speed, the maximum interval of differentiation being 32: 1. This means that the tempo of the slowest layer is expanded 32 times relative to its original tempo, while another layer is maybe five times slower. This is something I have only been able to do since the composition of SIRIUS: to *realize*, and *hear* and *experience* and *influence* the composition of multiple time-layers, during the act of composition.

In all my previous works of electronic music, like HYMNEN 'Anthems' I had to use very complicated machines like the Springer-machine for compressing or expanding material. The Springer-machine allowed material to be expanded or compressed in time without frequency transposition, or in pitch without changing the tempo, but only in a very primitive form. In some sections of KONTAKTE I had to splice it all by hand, which is an unbelievable labour. Imagine, I worked on the last section of KONTAKTE, beginning around 23′ 00″ or 24′ 00″, together with Gottfried Michael Koenig in Studio 11 on the third floor of Cologne Radio, for *three months*. And when it was completely ready, I spliced it together with the previous sections, listened, turned pale, left the studio and was totally depressed for a whole day. And I came back next morning and announced to Koenig that we had to do it *all over again*. I mean, he almost fainted.

You see, there is so much work involved in the synchronization of layers, and every sound in KONTAKTE is made in a very complicated way from speeded-up trains of pulses. We had to do it all over again because the general speed was too fast, the music was in too much of a rush. This meant we had to edit the whole section all over again, splicing hundreds, even thousands, of small segments of music. That mosaic technique was extraordinarily difficult, and also because you could only hear the result at the very end. If I had been using a synthesizer, as I did for SIRIUS, I would only have had to change the timescale, and I could have done this in one day, and been able to hear the result straight away, during the time of working.

RM: You have in the past expressed doubts about leaving the control or choice of a musical form to a machine. Are your views on the role of the computer in musical composition any different today, given the procedures now being worked out at IRCAM?

KS: This question comes at the right moment because I am in the midst of discussions with technical staff at Cologne Radio concerning the equipment for a new studio. For the first time we have a big budget for building a new studio: the old studio must move, and we are all agreed that the existing equipment is beginning to show its age and the Synthi 100 has never performed wholly satisfactorily, because it is terribly unstable and the filters are very bad. Rehberg in Stuttgart is willing to repair the Synthi 100 and also make us another one with the improvements we require, a fourth sequencer, and so on. In the meantime one of our collaborators has been to see a great many studios in America, and IRCAM in Paris, and I've been to IRCAM twice, for longer periods, to discuss with diGiugno all their future projects, and hear the results of everything that is possible up to the present time. I also talked at length with composers and former colleagues York Höller, Mesias Maiguashca and Rolf Gehlhaar about their experiences and work at IRCAM.

Having studied everything, including the new Buchla synthesizers and the latest Moog improvements, and also after an exchange of letters with Zinovieff, I have decided not to recommend diGiugno's apparatus or the method already being followed at IRCAM, for Cologne. What I want is a studio set up rather like an airplane cockpit, with at least four, if not six, keyboards: two or three at the right, and the same number at the left, with longer joysticks to control the moment of sounds, and potentiometers 30–40 centimetres long, to give much finer control of the voltages driving the sequencers. I want a machine that will simulate whatever generators, filters or transformers I may need, and I want it to respond instantly to the physical actions of my body, to the movements of my two hands on joysticks and keyboards and buttons, and, if possible, to my two feet on foot controls. I am not concerned with what kind of electronic brain drives it, as long as there is no perceivable time delay between what I am influencing and what I hear.

There should be at least four sequencers able to run simultaneously, with many more than 256 steps to each sequencer, so that I can make my musical sequences more differentiated and compose with many more layers. The multi-channel recording can be digital, if you like, but it is essential to keep the parameters separately accessible during synthesis. This is the crucial point. I want to be able to listen to a playback and say at a particular point, now I want to correct only the dynamics. I do not want to have to do the whole section over again. I do not mind if the parameters are simulated rather than real: dynamics, pitches, and timbres are what I think in, and I want to be able to continue to influence them separately until the result is completely finished. I would like even more parameters, for instance to control degrees of density and aleatoric distribution of musical events within defined limits. In fact, everything should be parametric. Meaning, there should be a button for it.

I have seen timecode autolocation in operation at Deutsche Grammophon: this is naturally an enormous step forward, to be able to go direct to a particular point on a tape just by calling up a number. Eliminating delays in studio work is an important aspect of digital recording. But the reduction of all the different parameters of music to one, to a single stream of digits, is unfortunate, because it means that if you want to change just a single aspect, of melody or timbre, you can't, because it has no separate existence. So what I want is analogue production, and I want any re-simulation also in analogue form, so that I can influence the parameters separately. After that, the recording can always be digital, I don't mind.

RM: Images of radio: of the composer as a radio receiver, and of music as messages from the beyond, feature repeatedly in your music and your commentaries about music. HYMNEN, OPUS 1970: KURZWELLEN MIT BEETHOVEN *'Short Waves with Beethoven', and* TRANS *spring to mind. How much does this radio imagery owe to your experiences as a youth?*

KS: Well, from the very few original sources we have, I know that Bach, Beethoven, Brahms, Stravinsky and a few other composers of the past have recognized the supremacy of intuition, based on the quality of the composer being a medium. He is a mouthpiece of the divine. So what you say is not only true for HYMNEN and KURZWELLEN MIT BEETHOVEN and TRANS, but also in INORI, or in particular for other works I have dreamed, like MUSIK IM BAUCH 'Music in the Belly'. But there are long stretches of HYMNEN which I simply heard inside me while composing, and which I was unable to incorporate into the musical structure at the time I received them. They had to be 'inserted' into the preconceived design. The whole *Einschub* 'insert' technique goes back to the KONTRA-PUNKTE and even to the DREI LIEDER 'Three Songs' when I first started composing. In particular the DREI LIEDER which I wrote very fast during the college vacation in 1950, and which is based directly on the overwhelming experience of inner sound visions which are stronger than your own will, technique, style preferences, or whatever it may be.

On the other hand, you are an engineer, you do mental

work, and there is sometimes a conflict between the two: you have overall visions, images which make demands of a kind you cannot yet realize, and they lead to the invention of new technical processes, but then the technical processes go their own way and become the starting point for other techniques which in turn provoke new intentions and you find yourself bombarded with images again. That is why I always take a divided sketchbook with me wherever I go: one section for general descriptions with words and designs, the other for musical notes, numbers, proportions, instrumental combinations.

This talk of inspiration is nothing new: Stravinsky talked about it, and there is a well-known opera by Pfitzner, *Palestrina*, where the composer is shown receiving music by divine inspiration, hearing it inwardly. Some of the claims for divine inspiration are frankly dubious, I must say, given the primitive or vulgar nature of the music which is produced. A memory stored in the psyche is sometimes taken for a cosmic influence. So this is a delicate subject to put into words, though I would say that inspiration is not just a childhood experience, but a continuing fact of life.

RM: I thought perhaps that listening to the radio as a child and at school might have impressed on you the idea of other cultures, and other freedoms being 'out there'?

KS: No, no, I didn't listen to the radio as a child. My father listened to the news and that was it. At boarding school in Xanten a group of us who were in the jazz band used to listen late at night to English army broadcasts of

American jazz music every now and then, which was forbidden. Not often: all in all perhaps ten times in four years. I don't think there was anything special in that.

RM: Were you ever aware that the wartime Frontberichte *news reports from the front line were studio creations using new tape technology?*

KS: No, I wasn't aware of this in the *Frontberichte* I heard at school: as far as I remember, there was mainly marching music at the beginning and end, a Wagner motif to announce the most important news items from the front, which were broadcast every once in a while, and then we used to hear just the voice . . . Aha! sometimes there were sound effects of airplanes. But I mean, the reality was much more interesting: every night I heard such sound effects for real.

The first impression I had of tape montage was when I was in Paris from the autumn of 1951 to the beginning of 1952, and heard the first examples of *musique concrète,* which were so unusual. That's it.

RM: The experience of working in a studio has brought new concepts of harmony, form and timing to music. Do you agree that studio training also alters the way you hear, and your sensitivity to sounds at different frequencies?

KS: Definitely. I have said I can't imagine any other colleague of my generation who has spent so many years and hours of his lifetime in a studio, and I have also done all the mixing of recordings of my music as well, which is very similar work. It took me practically four years in the studio to complete the composition and then the recording of SIRIUS: I mixed the recording combining the soloists and tape at least three times, and the last of these, for the stereo album, took almost three weeks. I am constantly in the studio listening, and certainly I have become aware that I hear much, much more than anybody else, simply because of the training. Quantitatively I hear more, and the result is that I hear more in the qualitative sense, much more polyphony. And when I feel something is wrong, I listen several times, and then I know exactly what it is: the overall dynamics, or a particular group of sounds, or a particular instrument whose level has to be brought up or down.

I am now so used to working with up to 24 faders simultaneously, and bringing certain instruments or voices in or out, that I can hear a difference of only 1dB in some cases, though everybody tells me, Herr Stockhausen, you're crazy, a change of 1dB cannot be heard, it is a waste of time. The DG people in Hannover have got used to the fact that I mark the fader positions sometimes up ½dB on a single channel, to get the balance completely right. It can take three hours, pushing faders back and forth, to know what I want for a take, say of thirty seconds: listening and performing on the mixing desk at the same time, like a player on a musical instrument. There are whole sequences lasting up to thirty minutes which are now in the electronic tape of SIRIUS, *uncut*, as the result of many, many attempts. The demands on one's listening ability are tremendous.

I also think playing in the Group Stockhausen has

contributed, having taken part as a performer in all the recordings of AUS DEN SIEBEN TAGEN, and in the many performances of FÜR KOMMENDE ZEITEN 'For times to come', which is music for which you do not need to read a score. The experience of closing the eyes completely, sometimes for as long as fifty minutes, and being only ears: this has developed my listening processes enormously. I don't mean physiologically or psychologically, I simply mean in terms of a total awareness: of the sound environment during a performance of four or five musicians who are all doing different things, and of the complexity of the sound.

RM: Without denying your commitment to a world music, would you agree that your music manifests a European, and specifically German sensibility and passion for order, while showing unusual openness to U.S. innovations in the arts? How strong, if any, are your links with the United States today?

KS: These are several questions at once. I would not agree that the passion for order, as you call it, is a specifically German sensibility or quality. I have found the restrictions involved in composing DER JAHRESLAUF 'The Course of the Years' for the Gagaku Ensemble, following a Japanese tradition derived via Korea from China, much more strict than any European or German tradition. The Noh theatre is much more strict, and the same is true for Indian music, and certainly true for Balinese music. It's a universal principle that music has always been very close to mathematics, only even more complex because it must be perceived aurally.

The other matter, concerning openness to U.S.

developments in the arts, is not specific. I think I am open to all developments and not just to those of America, however the opposite might be said about, how shall I put it, my confidence in the current trend in American art. The whole movement toward a so-called pop art, in the visual arts as well as in music, I see as a disaster, really shameful for mankind, once orientated toward the highest, whose only goal in art was to glorify the divine and the cosmic spirit, and for whom everything in the human world was related to these invisible worlds. That this is now replaced, generally speaking, by garbage art, which celebrates material impermanence and decay, is a disgrace. It needs a tremendous mysticism to adore God through garbage; it is possible, but when you reach a point where images of a lipstick or hot dog have the same significance as the crucifix or Madonna in earlier cultures, it shows where a country is heading spiritually.

And what is true of the content is equally true of the form, if you base a whole way of life on do-it-yourself, and deliberately choose to express yourself in disposable materials, which are by design and definition of inferior quality, perishable and even ugly. And this glorification of the banal and ugly is something we associate today to a large extent with American art and commerce, the much-maligned Coca-Cola culture, and I view it with sadness.

Apart from that, my relationships with America are very vivid: I am living with a wonderful American clarinet player, Suzee Stephens, I receive commissions from America, and have several times been teaching, performing and lecturing in the States for long periods. Then, America has also given me a great many students, all of them of a tremendous openness, so the country has many positive aspects.

RM: I rather thought there was a generally positive response in Europe after the war to the absence of tradition encountered in American arts.

KS: No, that's not true at all. I was there in 1958, if you can still call that after the war, and before that had been aware of what was going on in America through friends and contacts from about 1952. Boulez was there that year, on tour with Jean-Louis Barrault. I heard from him and other friends about abstract expressionism, and how it came about as a result of the influence of the Paris school of *tachisme.* This is my point: it was the French who triggered off the whole revolution of abstract expressionism with its Pollocks and Klines and dripping methods, all of which happened in a very short time in America, but which basically started, if you look back to its real origins, with Wols, a German painter who lived in Paris after the war, and who was the first to make paintings using dripping and scribbling and chance methods. And these paintings of Wols are closely related to certain paintings of Klee, only certain paintings, which also made use of similar aleatoric or tachistic techniques. So the claim that abstract expressionism is an entirely American phenomenon, which people now try to justify philosophically with talk about chance operations and the I-Ching and Zen Buddhism and so on — all this is only attempting to lay an American foundation for a European structure that had arrived ready-made.

As for an absence of tradition, what I encountered on

my tour of America in 1958 was a musical life and intellectual climate entirely dominated by German and Austrian immigrants. I found myself having to defend the young American school and their more free and aleatoric music against these extraordinarily strict and dogmatic professors and teachers who had moved to America and whose influence still pervaded the atmosphere of the music faculties. It was the same wherever I went: the climate was strongly deterministic, as a result of the influence of European scientists, and the musicologists were of the same orientation. It was against the domination of music by powerful academic forces that small groups of intellectuals reacted, stimulated by abstract expressionism, dadaism and surrealism. That's how it was. So one shouldn't be under any illusions about American culture and its origins.

RM: Does film mean a great deal to you, either as a representation of myth, or in a technical sense as structure? What is your attitude to film music, its orchestration and form?

KS: I'm not aware of orchestration and form; such things don't interest me very much while I'm watching a movie, no matter what is on screen. What I liked about films when I was younger, in wartime, was that they often made me weep, kept my eyes shining full of tears, because they were always about guys in submarines, being in love with their girls at home, going away and never seeing them again, but their love would go on for ever — this kind of fantastically idealized, fictional love made a deep impression on me. I can pick out very few films that I have liked since that time: like everybody else I enjoyed Chaplin's *The Gold Rush*, but I didn't like his other films so much, finding them exaggerated. The more successful he became, the more his films emphasized the sentimental side, and the formal side became weaker and weaker. I was also not impressed by the pie-throwing aspect of his earlier films, which is humour of a terribly primitive kind. But there was quality, here and there.

Some films have impressed me only after I became aware of moment-form in my own compositions. In Antonioni's *The Red Desert* for instance there is a scene where you are looking through the small window of a wooden cabin into the mist, when suddenly the bow of an enormous ocean liner moves silently past, very close, and only then do you realize that you are next to a canal. Or the shot of a light bulb against a white wall, hanging completely still on the left of the frame: that light bulb becomes so important from the fact that there is no camera movement at all, everything is conveyed in the stillness. Once film-makers discovered that film could stop as well as move, move at different speeds, and go from one extreme of total stillness to the other extreme of total movement, then to my mind the movies became interesting.

Blow-Up is another film I particularly like because it is concerned with processes of expansion and contraction similar to those I use in my music: you see a photographic image blown up just as I blow up my musical formulas, and the image is expanded to such an extent that you end up discovering figures in the detail that you would otherwise never see. This is a very musical idea, but it is only through having already made the discovery in my own work that I am able to recognize something like it in the film.

RM: There are musicians who specialize in accompanying silent movies, and their approach seems to have elements in common with your intuitive music, albeit in a rather primitive way. For instance, they respond directly to the screen image, without thinking, drawing automatically on a catalogue of music that is always at their fingertips.

KS: We did that once. It was after the last of three concerts the group gave in the courtyard of the Fondation Maeght in St Paul near Nice in France, which included an all-night performance of UNBEGRENZT 'Unlimited' from AUS DEN SIEBEN TAGEN. The owner of the foundation showed us a film of a French sculptor who makes welded sculpture in bronze, a very lively film, with fire and sparks like in a blacksmith's. I was asked to compose a score, but decided instead that our group should sit in front of the screen and play intuitively while the film was being shown. We gave ourselves a verbal direction, like a text from AUS DEN SIEBEN TAGEN, and watched the film and played, and they made a recording. Afterwards they suggested a second try, also to be recorded, but we said no, we would leave it at that. So that became the music for the film which is now fairly well known in the art world as a musical composition. But I don't think it was particularly well formed. It was very spontaneous in detail, but in other respects was simply led by the events on the screen: the musicians reacted like tourists being shown around, you see — Ha! and — Ho! and so on. Fortunately we had, as always, two sophisticated players in our group, one of whom, Harald Bojé, is very mean and aggressive, while the other, Aloys Kontarsky, has an extraordinary sense of humour. Really, a superb gift of repartee, and when you put them together with Johannes Fritsch, who can do superb animal imitations, amongst other things, on the viola, you have a good team, so there was a lot of humour in the performance. At times the music was a good deal wittier than the film. But it doesn't go much beyond musical conversation: it's not as deep or as rich in thought or form as my composed music.

RM: You have spoken of planning your music for reproduction by future technologies, for instance videodisc or holography, and it is evident that the visual choreography plays an increasingly important role in your music. How important is correct gesture and movement to the players' and the listener's understanding of your recent works?

KS: Correct gesture is absolutely vital in INORI because in this work the gestures correspond exactly to the intervals and proportions of the music. There is even a counterpoint between gesture and music. But I think gesture and dance are at the origin of music, and I certainly want to bring music back to that condition of ritual where everything you see is as important as what you hear, and not only the actions of producing the sound, but also those creating the music-theatre.

RM: In HARLEKIN 'Harlequin' for clarinet solo there is a composition of movement of the sounds in space, with the performer projecting the music in different directions.

KS: And in the opera LICHT all the time. I now compose the spaces in which I imagine my music being performed. Sounds are heard outside, then someone comes over a balcony, and then moves into the centre of the hall and sings a dialogue with another on the stage, and so on. The invisible choirs in DONNERSTAG aus LICHT 'Thursday from LIGHT' are much more important than the visible choirs. There are sixteen channels of polyphony sung by the invisible choirs, and in the First Act they are heard very far away as an undefinable acoustic horizon, while later in the Third Act the same choral music approaches and is heard in close-up, very close, from a circle of loud-speakers surrounding the public. When that happens, what you see on stage seems almost like a miniature projection of what you hear, which is invisible. So the visible world of the theatre and the invisible world of the angels and spirits, the invisible singers and choirs, are all developed in the opera to the same degree.

RM: Would you like to see improvements in the presentation of music on television, in terms of sound quality, stereophony, and the production and visualization of music?

KS: Obviously. At the Brussels World Fair of 1958 there were already television screens 1.5 metres square on show representing the domestic television of the future. Several times during the early sixties RCA proposed a television set on which it would be possible to see the person you were talking to on the telephone at the same time and on the same scale as real life. I imagine the television of the future being in a special room with a spherical screen extending at least 270° around and above the viewer, who will sit in a special chair in the centre. Image and sound will be transmitted in three dimensions. All my works since the seventies have been composed with this form of transmission very clearly in mind. The element of ceremonial, however, has been incorporated in my music for a much longer time. In KONTAKTE I describe how the tam-tam and gong are presented in the centre stage as objects on an altar, shining in a golden-red light from a special projector, and how at a certain time the players advance and strike them, and then go back to their places at the sides of the stage. MOMENTE too is practically an opera of Mother Earth surrounded by her chicks, and planning the stage actions and movements was very important. In Darmstadt during the late sixties I gave courses in composition with movement of players, walking, running, going in different directions, going into the forest, coming back from different directions, and so forth. It is clear to me that such movements will be included in future transmissions.

And only the most refined music-lover will choose to shut off the visual image, every now and then, and come back to a new kind of radio experience. People will come to realize that the eyes are needed only sometimes, and only for a more explicit perception, when the music and the movement are through-composed, as in INORI, which it would be a shame not to see. Personally, I would record a transmission on videocassette, and listen to the sound by itself, several times, in a darkened room, looking at the stars or with my eyes closed. After that I might enjoy playing it back from time to time with the picture. But the picture will certainly be transmitted, and for that reason it will have to be very carefully composed. The public will not put up any more with the same old faces and worn out postures of the opera establishment, or with camerawork that focuses on one dull hand gesture after another, no matter what is being sung, reaching out first with the left hand, then with the right hand, without any meaning. This inability to move among European performers will have to go: what is needed is gesture of great refinement, as in INORI or my opera LICHT.

RM: In SIRIUS *you make use of an eight-channel sound system for rotating sounds at 'strobe' speeds. Are you developing this innovation further?*

KS: Yes, I have taken it further in the choir piece for the new opera, called UNSICHTBARE CHÖRE 'Invisible Choirs'. There is a technical problem in that the rotation loudspeaker which I had built for SIRIUS is extraordinarily heavy. It weighs several tonnes, and stands in a heavy wire cage in an adjoining room with a notice 'Danger: Keep Out' on the door. No-one is allowed inside the room while the rotation speaker is switched on because if anything were to fly off the turntable while it was rotating, which can be at speeds up to twelve revolutions per second, such are the centrifugal forces that you could be killed outright.

I have looked for a replacement for this mechanical device but without success. EMS built equipment to simulate rotation but only with amplitude switching from one speaker to the next, no phase-shifting. And the phase-shifting in a moving sound is very subtle. I have not been able to find any solution to this and have had repeated discussions with the studio engineer. Control of phase-shifting in order to simulate sound movement in space is not yet technically possible. The design problems are too complex. There is no computer at present able to simulate the precise phase-shifting of sounds moving in several layers at once. Even to simulate the Doppler effect is a problem of enormous complexity. But with my rotating loudspeaker with eight microphones arranged round it in a circle, the effect is created automatically, and in addition, the turbulence created by the rotation is something very special, simulating exactly what happens when a racing car passes at speed.

So at the moment I don't see any alternative possibility for rotating sounds. Unfortunately the present machine is not the easiest to use, because it is operated by remote control, and the remote control is unreliable as a result of the enormous stresses placed on the electric circuits by the extreme changes of speed of rotation, from fast to slow and vice versa: it is liable to break down at any time.

RM: Is mixing a recording to stereo for commercial release a problem for you, given that so much of your music is intended to be heard in the round? Some of your recordings, such as HARLEKIN *and* MUSIK IM BAUCH *sound almost three-dimensional when one listens with headphones. How do you achieve this binaural effect with a multi-microphone recording?*

KS: For a long time now, since the second edition of KONTAKTE in 1968, I have mixed 4- or 8-channel recordings down to two-track in a very special way: I have reversed the phase of certain channels, which is very dangerous. Up to 1968 it was obligatory to issue all stereo recordings in mono-compatible form, but from the moment the technicians told me, Stockhausen, forget about mono-compatability, I have dared to incorporate phase reversal. For example, if I have sounds at the left of the stereo image, and mix in the same sounds with 180° phase-shift and a very precise change of dynamic on the other channel, it is possible to make them appear as though they are coming from behind. This use of phase reversal is normally forbidden in stereo recording: I sometimes lose the low frequencies because the signal and its reverse-phase image cancel out. But as long as the loss is within tolerable limits, the risk is worth taking. I can always boost the lower frequencies afterwards, of course. The result is that it becomes possible to simulate three-dimensional movement in sound with only two channels on a normal stereo recording.

I can even simulate sounds moving up the wall with only two fixed speakers. Not all sounds, you understand, only those of certain frequencies. And you have to cheat to given an impression of 'writing' with sounds vertically up and down the wall, or from front to back. The sounds should brighten in the high frequencies as they move upward, and lose brightness as they move downward. In this way an impression is created that the sound is moving up and down, because of the way our ears are constructed, and the way the sound reflections change depending on the distance of a source from the ground, house walls, trees and so on. I used to sit at my desk with my eyes closed and wonder how it was that I could hear the birds outside my window were flying up or down, high or low. After a while I perceived that the impression was due to changes in the brilliance of the sound, and so now, when I do the same thing in the studio: phase-shifting plus continuous changes of frequency and amplitude, I can get a similar effect.

RM: Traditional concert practice places the musicians at one end of a hall, and the audience in fixed seats at the other end. In some of your works, from GESANG DER JÜNGLINGE *to* INORI *and* SIRIUS *you have introduced movement and changes of perspective electronically, while in others, such as* MUSIK FÜR DIE BEETHOVENHALLE *'Music for the Beethoven Hall',* STERN-KLANG *'Star Sound',* HARLEKIN *and* ATMEN GIBT DAS LEBEN *'Breathing gives Life', the fixed perspective no longer seems to apply: the audience is allowed to move, or at least hear the music from different but equally legitimate perspectives. Is this breaking away from the traditional fixed perspective a factor in your proposals for new concert halls? Have your views on the subject changed at all since your involvement with the spherical German Pavilion at Expo '70, where the music moved round the audience?*

KS: MUSIK FÜR DIE BEETHOVENHALLE is not strictly a composition: I arranged a selection of my works to be performed simultaneously in three halls of the Beethoven Hall in Bonn. The performances were carefully timed to allow the public to make their own choice of programme and to move from one hall to another during the four hours of the evening. Within each hall the pieces were performed in the usual way, with the audience seated on the floor on comfortable rugs; they would listen in absolute silence and only move after a piece was finished.

I had arranged for the intermissions between items to coincide for all three halls, to allow the public to move from one to another as they wished. The idea was that my music should be experienced like exhibits in a museum, and that those who already knew certain pieces should be able to choose to listen to others they did not know. It worked very well, and is still a model for a new performance practice.

Of course, I included a new composition, FRESCO 'Wall Sounds for Meditation' for five orchestral groups, which lasts for over five hours, and was performed in the lobbies of the large complex of the Beethoven Hall, starting an hour before the beginning as the audience began to arrive and continuing throughout the evening until after they had gone home. The five groups were seated along the corridor walls and would be playing as the listeners passed by.

STERNKLANG is park music: the work is performed by five instrumental groups widely separated in a park, and the audience is free to move around during the performance. But it has become obvious to me, over the many performances I have directed, that as the evening wears on — a performance lasts about three hours, from 9 to 12 in the evening, on a summer night, with full moon — people move about less and less, preferring to lie on the grass, and listen to one group for twenty minutes or half an hour, and then maybe move to another group. They begin to understand that it doesn't matter where you are, what is important is to hear the spatial depth of many layers of music at different distances.

HARLEKIN must be performed and danced on a stage, and the audience should not move during the performance. To perform STIMMUNG 'Tuning' and other pieces involving loudspeakers, it is possible to have the performers in the middle of the audience. STIMMUNG we have often performed with the six singers in a circle on a podium 1.10 metres high in the centre of the hall with the audience seated around, and the effect is very good for this piece. Similarly for performances of HYMNEN with soloists, and for KURZWELLEN we arrange the speakers rather high in a circle around the public. But in all these cases the public is not moving. The only pieces, besides STERNKLANG and FRESCO, where the public was allowed to promenade, were those which made up ALPHABET FÜR LIÈGE 'Alphabet for Liège', which again was like a series of exhibits in a museum; there were fourteen rooms, and the audience moved from room to room, from one exhibit to the next, and could always hear the music: there were no closed doors, and the rooms were arranged like a labyrinth.

ATMEN GIBT DAS LEBEN is a real choir opera, on a stage in front of an audience, and it is viewed from the front, just as for HARLEKIN, because at the climax Harlequin advances to the footlights and kneels down in front of the public.

But there are other pieces of mine where the audience is surrounded by musicians, like GRUPPEN for three orchestras and CARRÉ for four choirs and orchestras; sometimes the listeners face into the centre as well. For all of my electronic works, and for SIRIUS the public faces the centre, and in SIRIUS the performers are outside the public.

Stereo listening is the product of a very brief period of history. It started towards the end of the Renaissance with private performances, before invited guests, of Greek drama in the houses of the nobility. The rooms were fairly small, which meant that the audience had to sit in a certain area and the performers were confined to a separate part of the room. In Bologna there is still a wonderful palace on the top of a hill, and as soon as I saw the terrace, with a lawn in front enclosed by a semi-circular hedge, I said immediately what a fantastic setting it would be for my music. I imagined the kinds of entertainments, with costumes and dancing, that were given there in former times: performances of theatre and opera, where the players would come and go by different doors, disappear into the surrounding hedges and then come back from a different direction. There are many little renaissance and baroque theatres in Vienna, Salzburg, Würzburg, Kassel and other German cities, which show a whole variety of stage and seating arrangements. The concert hall is a much more recent phenomenon.

Then, naturally, I am all for ritual. I think the Catholic mass is fantastic musical drama, a highly articulate play, and musical ritual. I think of the rituals in Bali, in India — I have heard many different versions of the *Ramayana*, also rituals in Africa (and I don't mean only the folk rituals, but also the more developed esoteric rituals, like those of the Dogon priests). In Japan you often have Noh plays presented in a park, on a typical Noh stage, with the audience sitting round in the open.

So music in the future will be performed a lot more in the open air, I think, as it was a long time ago. And if it isn't possible to perform in the open, then inside larger auditoriums, suitably transformed. That is what I did in

1980, when a performance of STERNKLANG that was to have taken place in the Bonn Rheinauen park, had to be moved into the Beethoven Hall because of rain. We had planned it for two years, for a night with a full moon, and two days before the scheduled performance it rained so hard that we had to move into the Beethoven Hall, which is some 50 metres long and 25 metres wide. We transformed the hall into a park. I asked for 250 potted trees of all kinds, high and low, to be brought in; I also had rugs laid down, some of them 25 metres long, so that the public would not make any noise. And we gave two performances, one for nearly two thousand, the other for an audience of over a thousand young people. I have published a complete documentation of this presentation of STERNKLANG indoors, with photographs and plans, as an addendum to the score.

I transform the interior of an auditorium fairly regularly, when we do STERNKLANG, and also SIRIUS, which is not always performed in the cloisters of a church, but sometimes in a gymnasium, as at Metz, or atriums, which happened in America, and then I ask for tall plants to be brought inside to create a pleasant atmosphere.

My opera LICHT also creates great difficulties of staging, because it is not at all traditional in that sense. It takes some adjusting to La Scala, or to any opera house, when there are things going on in the balconies, performers coming in from the back and from all sides, when you hear sounds from the aisles and moving along the corridors outside the auditorium, and added to that a circle of loudspeakers contributing an extra dimension of multi-layered depth of perspective to the acoustic experience. My music gives many examples of different ways of treating music spatially, because aural perspectives in multiple layers, one layer behind another, are very important to me.

Concert halls should develop in an entirely new way in future. They should be circular, or nearly circular — say octagonal, in shape; there should be no fixed balconies and galleries for the public, but a gallery for musicians or loudspeakers, or both, one about 1.10 metres high, a second one about 3.50 metres high, all around, fully wired for microphones and amplification. The public seating should ideally be movable. There should be three stages at least, to the left, front and right, but interconnected, so that one stage can be in preparation while another carries the action, also to allow up to three scenes to be played simultaneously around a 270° arc. Then if it happened that, if you were paying close attention to one part of the action and missed something going on elsewhere, you could come back again to experience what you had missed. The element of theatrical polyphony is important in my works, and the new halls should be designed for it.

I have also made many sketches for larger auditorium complexes to be sited near shopping centres, offering continuous music programmes with intermissions every twenty or twenty-five minutes for the public to be admitted, so people would go and listen to some spatial music for a while, and then go away again, individually, in their own time, as to a movie. In another studio you would have live performances at certain times throughout the day: for example, you might have a certain team of players appearing for a month-long season and giving performances at 10am, 12 noon, 2pm, 4pm and 6pm daily, then the next month you would have a different team, playing my music, and so on, permanently. I have described this in detail many times.

In the larger auditorium complexes there should be at least three main halls of different sizes, so that simultaneous programmes can be presented, or compositions which involve several different spaces and sizes of ensemble. You could then start a performance in one hall, then proceed, led by the players, to another to allow a change of scene; it would be possible to alternate large and small ensembles, with in between the larger items soloists performing in alcoves, as we did in the caves of Jeita in the Lebanon.

I have described the procedure for synchronizing multiple performances in relation to the MUSIK FÜR EIN HAUS 'Music for a House' performance which was organized under my direction at Darmstadt in 1968. Three floors of the Freemasons' Lodge were synchronized. In a basement room you could hear everything that was happening, but only indirectly, over loudspeakers; once you mounted the stairs and entered a room, you could only hear what was being performed in that particular room, except at certain times when for synchronization purposes loudspeakers transmitted what was being played elsewhere. So this was a case of a building with its different rooms becoming a representation of the different layers of a polyphonic composition, the audience being able to pass from layer to layer of the music, by moving from room to room, which is a very interesting experience.

In another design, access is by a spiral ramp outside the building, and from the top it is possible to look down into rooms on several different levels, which can be reached by a network of connecting gangways. The rooms and gangways are acoustically treated so that the public is able to move from place to place without making a disturbance.

There is an old temple site of the Aztecs on Monte Alban near Oaxaca in Mexico, which has given me a lot of ideas. It's an enormous oval on the flattened top of an entire hill, and I learned from reading about the site that during great rituals involving many thousands of participants, the few priests were able to give an impression of being there in much greater numbers. The temple had a number of raised altars, several hundred metres apart: a group of priests would appear at one altar, then after a while all but one of them would disappear, and run through a network of underground passages to another altar. In this way they were able to keep the ceremony going continuously at a great number of altars with only a dozen or so priests shuttling in secret from place to place underground, giving the impression that they were in their hundreds. It gave me the idea for musical rituals, where the musicians would disappear and reappear somewhere else, in a similar way.

RM: Since the seventies your music has become increasingly contrapuntal, as distinct from polyphonic, almost as though the musical 'atoms' of your earliest works have evolved into organic molecules which are now linking up in increasingly complex ways. Is contrapuntal a fair description, and would you agree that your greater interest in melody is helping to make your recent music more accessible to the general public?

KS: On reflection I think both observations are true. Through composing with formulas I have become more precise in counterpoint, by which I mean note to note relationships within a small-scale region of pitch and time, up to about a minute. It comes about because I am working with formulas and combining them to make a so-called superformula. Every interval counts, in order that the listener can follow each formula very precisely. To take a particular example, in SIRIUS, when I worked with sequencers, there are sometimes as many as 3x3 lines heard simultaneously, and every note is exactly placed in relation to every other note that is either simultaneous with it or immediately adjacent, that is, in respect to a scale of harmonic complexity between consonance and dissonance, or growth and decay of harmonic functions.

On the other hand, I have also extended the idea of polyphony more than ever. If we think back to GRUPPEN for three orchestras, or ZEITMASZE, where there are passages where every instrument is playing at a different speed, sometimes extraordinarily different, by a factor of 1:16 subdivisions of a time unit. If we compare these with MANTRA, MUSIK IM BAUCH, and INORI, the timescale of the polyphony is enormously increased in the later works. In MUSIK IM BAUCH for example, a single instrument like the marimbaphone, with two players, has one musical formula from the TIERKREIS 'Zodiac' cycle spread out over twenty-eight minutes: if you want to hear it, you need the ears of a giant, and the memory of a giant, otherwise you will not be able to tell if a wrong note is played, or at the wrong time, they are spread so far apart. Future generations will really have to expand their perception in order to be aware of a melody which unfolds over such a long time. It is the same for INORI: sometimes the formula is spread over four minutes, or even longer, in just one layer. Then layers are superimposed: in MANTRA up to four layers are superimposed in the two piano parts, the largest expansion being about four minutes, which may be heard simultaneously with another layer of two two-minute expansions in succession, or a sequence of four one-minute expansions, down to the shortest mantra which lasts only 3½ seconds: the same formula always in many different expansions and vertical combinations.

You can switch attention from one layer to another, and perceive the same work on a different timescale, even more so in INORI, in which the formal divisions of the work represent one statement of the formula extended over seventy minutes, and for each subdivision of the form down to the smallest unit there is a further contraction of the formula. The same principle is now guiding the composition of my opera LICHT: the basic statement of the superformula stretches over the entire week, its seven subdivisions or 'limbs' being allocated one to each of the seven evenings, in all a total of something more than twenty hours of music. Each evening's opera, lasting between one and a half and four hours, represents only one section of the superformula; then again there is a statement of the formula encompassing every evening, and further statements of the formula for every scene. In the scene LUZIFERS TRAUM on which I am working at the moment, there is one statement of the formula for Lucifer which extends over about twenty-eight minutes, which is the length of the scene, beginning on middle D flat. Over that is superimposed a sequence of five further statements of the Lucifer formula, in the bass, beginning on the five notes of an element from the beginning of the SAMSTAG 'Saturday' limb of the superfomula: A flat, A, B flat, B, C sharp. During the same time period the formula for Eva repeats eight times, giving a ratio of 1: 5: 8 among the layers. Finally, the Michael formula is represented by just one note throughout the entire twenty-eight minutes, a single statement of the high F which is the Saturday segment of Michael's formula for the whole week, and which appears here as a pre-echo. Here, and in every scene in the opera, the layer-composition is even more thorough than in MUSIK IM BAUCH, INORI or MANTRA. MICHAELS JUGEND, to take another example, is sixty-one minutes long, and represents a single statement of the Michael formula, and in the interval between each note of the formula a further statement of the formula is heard. Or take EXAMEN 'Examination', the examinations of Michael, which form the third scene of MICHAELS JUGEND: the three examinations he undergoes are again articulated by statements of the formula, based on the central notes of the superformula. So the whole work is really built, as you say, as a molecule is built out of atoms, or a human being from cells, a solar system from the earth and other planets, or a galaxy from stars.

RM: Have you considered extending the range of expansion and contraction of a formula by electronic means, where the actual speeds become too fast or too slow for human players?

KS: That is happening all the time in SIRIUS: the

sequences are speeded up to 100 times a second, so naturally the formula goes into noise. You hear such transitions all the time, from continuous sound to fast rhythmic oscillations, then at the other extreme pulses slowed down to such an extent that they become a steady note, when the timescale is so expanded that there is something like twenty or thirty seconds from one attack to the next. It is certainly true that the synthesizer is needed to make smooth transitions in such cases.

RM: How are today's students to be trained in these new musical skills? Should music courses incorporate sound recording, for instance?

KS: I think every musician who wants to compose should not only spend a certain amount of time in a recording studio, but also do regular work in a studio. I cannot imagine a composer making important advances in the future without a full knowledge of studio techniques. Performers too, like my two sons Markus and Simon, should be thoroughly informed about recording techniques: have their own equipment, record themselves constantly, do their own mixing and supervise the recordings of their own playing. Recording should be regarded in the same way as playing the piano in earlier times, as an essential part of every musician's training. Of course, the métier is expanding: everyone should still learn piano as well as their major instruments.

RM: Some would argue that for a musician, recording skills are different in kind from live performance skills.

KS: True. But then you learn to switch skills. Markus, for example, likes studio multi-track recording very much, and at the same time he is an excellent concert trumpet player, and also an excellent improviser on jazz trumpet. Sometimes he improvises for three or four hours in a jam session, and then plays my music with me; and when he does solo recording, he takes complete charge of the recording, using the playback technique of recording one layer at a time. Players should not be inhibited from learning a new technique, or limit themselves to only one approach to music making. Ideally they should know the complete range of performance skills, and recording too.

RM: I have given you a list of subjects normally studied in a college music course. Which of them would you retain, and what new features would you like to see added?

KS: I had to ask myself the same question in planning the Cologne New Music Courses: what I should organize for the students, whom I should hire to give courses, and so on. My first decision then, was to devote a major part of the course, two or three sessions of three hours per week, to *Hörbildung*, training in listening. This would involve listening to something you don't know at all, from a tape recording, then transcribing it in the way phonetics students at university transcribe an unfamiliar African dialect. As you remember, this course was a great struggle for everybody, to find an adequate notation; most of the students did not have absolute pitch and were constantly having to run back and forth to the next room to check the pitch with a tuning fork or some such device, or to measure the time with a stopwatch. So for such a course students should be provided with separate cubicles, each one furnished with playback equipment and headphones, a keyboard, a metronome and a stopwatch, and spend an hour and a half or two hours there each day re-running the tape as often as they like, and transcribing it. That's how I worked when I transcribed the entire tape of HYMNEN into score form, and SIRIUS, which took me three months to transcribe after having worked it out on the synthesizer.

Transcription of this kind is the best basic training of all for a musician, because this way a student really begins to listen, and becomes aware of what musicianship is all about. For this reason there should be a specialist teacher of transcription, one able equally to demonstrate classical music transcriptions, for which a score already exists, or transcription using an alternative form of notation, as I employ in the electronic score of KONTAKTE. In the Cologne Courses I used to record and transcribe short sections of short wave broadcasts of completely unfamiliar material. So in addition to learning an instrument all students should be given this essential basic training in audio education.

Training in singing or playing a chosen instrument is naturally most important. A lesson of two hours a week for your instrument or voice, or better still, lessons in both singing and instrument for everyone. As a student in Cologne I used to sing in the choir as well as taking piano lessons, and before that in the school at Xanten I studied violin and oboe as well, which was very useful. It should be a *sine qua non* that every music student learn to sing as well as play.

Analysis is important, but it should be analysis through listening. Learning to transcribe will already teach students a great deal about phrasing and timing, and the relationship of smaller and larger elements of form. Of course you can build on this by specialist reading and tuition, but I would avoid overloading analysis with too many words and diagrams: one should always be able to hear what is being talked about by the use of frequent musical examples between comments. Analysis without hearing the music is a meaningless exercise. To do it properly requires an enormous effort on the part of the teacher, in preparing the tapes of short excerpts. I know, having broadcast analyses of the music of Webern, Debussy, Bartók, my own music, Boulez, Nono: I would always play the exact section of music I was talking about, sometimes repeating the same one or two bars six or eight times, with barely a sentence between, to draw attention to specific features of the music.

Composition: yes, but only for those who want to compose. But how is it to be taught? That is the question. A short while ago I gave a composition course in Rome with lasted eighteen days. There were around 120 participants of whom about thirty were actively involved in desk work for two hours every afternoon. I prepared a big wall-chart showing the superformula of DONNERSTAG aus LICHT, four metres long, and colour-coded; I explained how it was composed, and from the second day everybody had to write their own formula. After that I would analyze their work every day for an hour or an hour and a half, and make criticisms. They would write their own formulas large-scale in front of the class so that everybody could see, and I played them over and over on the piano, and I would criticize what I thought were bad pitches, bad rhythms, bad dynamics, bad pauses, and so on. So the course was designed to teach students to compose formulas, and a follow-up course would show them how to treat the formulas and generate larger forms from them.

Amateur choir: yes; orchestra: very important. The course you outline here is really what you should find in a good conservatory of music. It could be worthless or excellent training for a musician, depending on the conservatory. A good conservatory can be hard to find.

Acoustics: that's extraordinarily important. It's never taught properly: the course should be given by someone who also has qualifications in phonetics, so that there isn't too much talk only in terms of pendulums and numbers, but real acoustic instruction and audio-analyses of actual sounds. You start by analyzing stationary sounds, musical and vocal, and move on gradually to analysis of less stationary sounds; in that way you discover what acoustics is all about. While I was composing KONTAKTE I spent months in tape recording instrumental sounds and then analyzing them using filters: marimbaphone notes, drum notes, cowbell notes, making a complete breakdown of the attack and envelope characteristics of each one, and drawing them in detail on graph paper. In this way I became gradually aware of the inner structure and evolution of a sound. To have sound analysis, as I call it, as part of an acoustics course, is very important.

Orchestration: is basically hopeless unless you constantly refer to recorded extracts from selected compositions when you explain the range of instruments and their dynamic possibilities. To tell students about the ranges of instruments is done in a month, and if they forget they've only themselves to blame, because there are plenty of books available. Be sure to tell them the best books: that's a great help for a start.

However, there is not a single book which talks about the *relative* dynamics of instruments, and this is the most important aspect of orchestration. Strauss, in his 1905 revision of the Berlioz text on orchestration, gives examples of orchestral pieces, which is good, but I have never yet seen a book which explains why, in a certain score, one instrument can play *piano* and be in balance with another instrument playing *forte* at the same time; or advise whether the composer should write *piano* for the one, and *forte* for the other, or whether both should be written *piano* and the conductor should decide that the other should play *forte* for the sake of balance.

This whole question of dynamics is a major issue in orchestration. To my mind, dynamics is the most difficult parameter in composition. Almost all the corrections I still make after decades of experience as a composer, and having spent so many hours in rehearsing and recording, are in the field of dynamics. Even when I balance the dynamics of electronic music and live instruments for performances of works like KONTAKTE, or HYMNEN with soloists, or SIRIUS, where I already have complete control over the dynamics of the electronic part, in the final sound projection it comes down to very fine adjustments which make all the difference to the total sound image. The dynamics are always having to be adjusted: my personal scores of KONTAKTE, SIRIUS and STERNKLANG are all marked in red, green and yellow, mainly for changes of dynamics. After I have composed a piece, the moment I go into a rehearsal the dynamics go into the balance: I simply cannot foresee completely how they will sound in practice. I have to work out in sound what I have heard in my mind and written, basically mindful that some instruments mask others, and that either the one that is too prominent may have to be taken down a little, or the other one brought up. Naturally that changes the predetermined scheme of the composition to a certain extent, but I have to do it.

RM: But when you alter the balance at a mixing desk, the timbre of a particular dynamic is not affected, surely?

KS: Sometimes, sometimes not. At times, for the sake of clarity, I have to raise the level of an entire part, because it doesn't make sense to require people to break their necks to sing something very complicated and painstaking, and then have nobody able to hear it. And that often means making sacrifices elsewhere, bringing down parts which are already very satisfactory in order that others can be clearly heard at the same time. You just cannot know completely how the balance will work out, until you hear it in practice.

RM: And what about notation?

KS: That's already covered in the transcription course. Immediately you start on transcription, you are involved in notation, your main topic of conversation is notation, how to find the right sign for the sound. Then you should study the scores of composers you can trust — they are very few, by the way — who know what they are doing when they write *staccato* or *portato*, or *legato*; who know what the signs really mean, and also the meaning of a rest. They should learn that in a Stockhausen score a note should not be shortened before a rest, but held *exactly* to the value that is written. Notation should be studied in particular scores, and only in those scores, otherwise you get totally confused.

RM: Would you recommend any in particular?

KS: My scores; I can't think of any others I would want to recommend. Sometimes, when I look at a Boulez score, I want to tear my hair, the music is so over-determined: you ask yourself what does this accent mean on top of a short note which already has a precise duration and a *fortissimo* indication, and is written for piano as well? The music is sometimes so overloaded with signs, and yet Boulez is one of the sharpest minds.

*RM: Stravinsky once complained (*Conversations with Igor Stravinsky, *London, 1959, p. 120) of his difficulty in persuading orchestral players on occasion to interpret crotchets marked* portato *as* sforzato *and* staccato *semiquavers with accents, depending on the style.*

KS: Then he should specify. I don't agree with that at all. I don't want any accents if I do not write accents. There is only one exception, and that is when I write music where the time signature is changing. Not the early works: KREUZSPIEL, SPIEL for orchestra, or SCHLAGTRIO 'Percussion Trio', where the barline is only for synchronization purposes, but those works where a change of bar-length indicates a change in the stress pattern. In such cases the normal stress patterns apply: strong, weak, medium, weak, and so forth. One should study very carefully the meaning of the symbols in specific scores. My scores are, I think, exceptionally rational in their use of notation. So if some textbook tells you always to play *staccato* so that it lasts half of the written value, I say nonsense: in my music a *staccato* is always short, no matter what the note value. If I had a precise duration in mind, I would write a precise value.

And then, finally, I would recommend that every student of music go dancing at least once a week. *And dance*. Please, really dance: three or four hours a week. Any dance, whatever is going at the discothèque or dance spot, though discos tend to become monotonous. Different dances; you should dance with a partner, and to different rhythms and tempi: slow, medium, fast, and in different rhythms based on two, three or four beats. Make your own evenings with tapes of folk dances: Austrian, Spanish, Hungarian, South American. There should be a good dancing teacher on the staff, that would be perfect: not for ballet, but for social dancing, real social dancing, once a week, as part of the music course, for the whole duration of study.

Social dancing, singing and playing an instrument, listening training. And then, only then, if you please, do you begin little by little with what is called 'tonal counterpoint', 'tonal harmony', 'history of music'. History of music *last*, please, at the very end. 'Study of past styles': *last*: in the final year perhaps. Because all you have to do is tell them what books there are, and if they want to then they can read the books; you don't need to talk too

much about that, there are plenty of excellent books and
records available. Let those who are interested in history
do it, and those who are not interested do something else:
they will still be well-trained musicians.

AFTERWORD
Beauty and Necessity
by Robin Maconie

There is a view of twentieth-century art as the expression of individual wilfulness. To those for whom the function of classical art is to maintain and not to question social attitudes, the message of much of present-day art is frankly subversive. Anarchy of course has its place. It is entertaining; it is fun: and the corollary of that is that it should not be taken seriously. The free world is quick to condemn political dictatorships which practise censorship of artistic expression. But among democracies the idea that art, and modern art in particular, is merely decorative or merely entertaining can also be seen as a subtler, but no less potent propaganda device, to render new ideas ineffectual.

A composer today may be ruled by public opinion and hope for material success as an entertainer, or strive to lead it and be condemned to a life in the shadow of poverty and public scepticism. Many of the greatest composing influences of the past hundred years have paid for their musical principles in physical and material suffering. There are no public memorials for the sacrifices of a Schoenberg, a Webern, a Varèse, a Bartók. Instead, the familiar indifference of Western bureaucracies toward living artists is explained away by the cynicism that great art is necessarily born of personal adversity, or the complacency that it is for future generations to decide whether an artist is deservedly or undeservedly left in the lurch.

Composers subsidize their primary activity by concertizing as performers or conductors. A very few, Boulez and Stockhausen among them, have challenged the inertia of the music industry and the media, forcing them to treat their music and the ideas it represents with the consideration they deserve. Thanks to them the new music scene has become a healthier and more principled environment in recent years.

As Aaron Scharf has shown (in *Art and Photography*, London, 1978), underlying the extraordinary flowering of aesthetic diversity among the visual arts during the nineteenth and twentieth centuries is a newness of vision, of ways of seeing the world, which has a great deal to do with the discoveries of photography. Not so much in the trivial sense of the camera becoming the artist's sketchbook, as in it extending the artist's range and scale of vision beyond the ordinary limits of unaided human discrimination. The scientific vision of Eadward Muybridge's pioneering photographic images of human beings and animals in motion has provided artists from the time of Degas and Rodin to Francis Bacon today with an inspirational store of templates from nature of an accuracy and momentary precision inaccessible to the unaided eye. Often it is the immediacy of the image which is its most poetic feature: at the same time instantaneous and dynamic, balanced and unbalanced, suspended and in transition. In addition to discriminating in time, the camera can also respond to nuances of tone beneath the threshold of ordinary sight. It was thanks to Daguerre's remarkable invention that Turner was able to see the image of the sky over Paris as a visible substance modulated in light, and which stimulated him to make the quantum leap from being an eighteenth-century painter of neoclassic landscapes to becoming a transcendental visionary proclaiming the elemental forces of wind and sky.

Technology extends human perceptions, and to communicate the idea of extended perception is frequently as important, and sometimes more important, than the representation of a recognizable object in the field of vision. As Klee said, art does not render the visible, rather it makes visible. Technology reveals new images which are not only exciting in themselves but as intuitions of new perceptual powers. Both Kandinsky's early watercolour improvisations and Malevich's suprematist drawings not only convey images of changed perspectives — in the former case, of the world as seen through a microscope, in the latter as seen by aerial photography — but in addition, these almost disarmingly casual, even accidental images are charged with a feeling of a profoundly and permanently altered consciousness. Instead of holding up a mirror to nature, the new art fashions a lens through which nature can be viewed from radically different perspectives.

In a similar way, the miniature compositions produced around 1910 by Webern, Schoenberg, Stravinsky, Ravel and others also suggest a radical shift of aural perception provoked by acoustic recording. As with the camera, so too the impact of new technology on the art of music has its superficial aspect, to be found among the folklorists who used the phonograph as a sketchpad to capture musical images from nature to be worked up at leisure into 'art' compositions. By its far greater intensity of expression, however — and notable avoidance of folklore — the creative impulse underlying such compositions as Schoenberg's *Herzgewächse*, Stravinsky's Japanese Lyrics and the orchestral sets by Webern seems to respond, both in timescale and in refinement of instrumental treatment, to an intuition more profound than a taste for haiku.

It was an intuition transcending the limitations of the medium, and yet conditioned by them. In the early years of the twentieth century, phonograph recording was one of the wonders of the age. The sound was typically feeble, noisy and shortlived: even so, it inspired a music of economy of gesture and refined intimacy of expression. The substantial emotional charge, however, lay elsewhere, in the idea that this most ephemeral experience of human expression could be stored and reproduced exactly and at any desired time. That simple idea had enormous implications for the direction of musical development, and for classico-romantic symphonic values. Suddenly formal criteria long regarded as absolute, such as repetition and recapitulation, question and answer, and the logical continuity of first-movement form, could be seen as symptomatic of all-too-human limitations of aural perception and recall.

Recording sowed the idea of a renewed intimacy and subtlety of expression. Repeated hearings of a recording implied a concentration of utterance which no longer needed repeats at crucial intervals, or to unfold in a logical way at the pace of the slowest member of the audience. It both made a virtue of economy and, through published examples of the voices of famous celebrities and 'sound pictures' combining music and naturalistic sound effects, inspired new artistic freedoms to imitate the atonal melodic cadence of natural speech, and to combine music and noise as equal elements in a new form of aural art. Suddenly the ultimate logic of symphonic development, desirability of employing large numbers of musicians, and divine right of diatonic convention, no longer seemed the only legitimate options.

Varèse was a composer who saw his activity as an essential contribution to human knowledge. He challenged the propriety and wisdom of contemporary society to deny composers the same rights and subsidies available to the scientist or engineer in the field of acoustics and communication. The kind of collaborative relationship Varèse sought to establish with Bell Telephone Laboratories during the thirties — a relationship the conductor Stokowski proved to be both feasible and useful in a famous series of experiments in stereophonic and multichannel recording — was finally realized during the seventies with the establishment in Paris under Boulez of a research institute in which composers, performers, scientists and engineers participate in a disciplined joint programme for the advancement of musical and acoustical science.

Technology can create images which are themselves

exciting, and it can also suggest new ways of generating images which, because they are self-sufficient and unanswerable to traditional ideas of taste, lead to exciting and revealing results. The arts have long been engaged in an endeavour to reconcile classical determinism (representing human responsibility for the natural world) with procedures leading to unpredictable but recognizably characterized results (reflecting natural processes which are beyond human prediction or total control). This attention to chance and the superrational — or 'chaos' as it is now popularly known — is as old as the science of statistics, and is at last attracting wider public investigation and debate as a subject of recreational computing.

Both Xenakis and Cage have sought in their different ways to compose systems of choice reflecting indeterminate processes in nature, or mathematical strategies for defining them. Their music is a reflection of the fact that indeterminate processes from stocks and shares to the weather are among the realities of contemporary social organization but remain beyond the reach of classical description in musical terms. It is interesting to note that in mainland Europe, where composing is taken seriously, a book on the philosophy of new music can be published under the title of *Par volonté et par hasard*, in German *Wille und Zufall*, but in its English version is simply called *Pierre Boulez in conversation with Célestin Deliège*. In such small ways is music kept in its place in the English-speaking world.

Compared to the work of his contemporaries, Stockhausen's music has a depth and rational integrity that is quite outstanding. There is not a single aspect or degree of indeterminacy that he has not investigated and assimilated. His researches, initially guided by Meyer-Eppler, have a coherence unlike any other composer then or since. He has discovered and refined a whole new notational language. He has mastered the technologies of the recording studio and electronic tone synthesis. As Stravinsky said, one never thinks of Beethoven as a superb orchestrator because the quality of invention transcends mere craftsmanship. It is the same with Stockhausen: the intensity of imagination gives rise to musical impressions of an elemental and seemingly unfathomable beauty, arising from necessity rather than conscious design.

What we call beauty is normally associated with perceived order. It is a human order, since nature is represented in ways designed to flatter human scales and sensitivities or perceptual discrimination. Underlying the emotional charge associated with the recognition of images as beautiful is the idea of human authority over an unruly creation. By depicting creation as intelligible, the artist represents the observable universe as the natural dominion of humankind. It follows that part of the emotional charge associated with an impression of beauty is the sense of power which comes with the intuition of a clearer understanding of the pattern of nature, and arising from that, the desire to possess and rule.

By contrast, the beauties revealed by technology suggest aesthetic neutrality and deliberate non-intervention in the pattern of nature. One does not ask the stars to assemble in ordered rows, or bacteria to move in step. These images are somehow inherently pleasing: the aesthetic satisfaction comes from the quality of imagery, not necessarily from the image itself. We can even alter our criteria of aesthetic satisfaction to accord with the implications of image quality, so that a blurred impression which might appear false in a still life becomes pleasing when associated with an intention to convey movement.

How then is classical aesthetics, based on a humanized distortion of nature, to be reconciled with the contrary aesthetic of accepting images as talismans of uncorrupted natural processes? How is the sense of beauty associated with the idealized nature of a Botticelli to be compared with the sense of beauty associated with an art which imitates images of charged particles in collision or galaxies in formation? All intuitions of beauty may be reconciled as images of extended perception, expressed overtly in the orderly simplifications of classical representation, and implicitly in the revealed complexities of abstraction. Even at its most contrived, chaos should appear natural. There are consistencies in the distribution of the stars, in the texture of foliage and in the formation of clouds.

The time will come when Stockhausen's contribution is universally recognized. Not for his music in itself—that is already happening — but for the 'mental work': what the generation of Helmholtz once acknowledged as musical science.

APPENDICES

Suggested further reading

The following is a list of texts in English which are relatively non-technical and may be found in music libraries.

Cott, Jonathan, *Stockhausen: Conversations with the Composer*, London, 1974

Ernst, David, *The Evolution of Electronic Music*, New York, 1977.

Griffiths, Paul, *A Concise History of Modern Music*, London, 1978.

Griffiths, Paul, *A Guide to Electronic Music*, London, 1979.

Harvey, Jonathan, *The Music of Stockhausen*, London, 1975.

Maconie, Robin, *The Works of Karlheinz Stockhausen*, 2nd edition, London, 1989.

Manning, Peter, *Electronic and Computer Music*, London, 1984.

Stockhausen, Karlheinz, 'Actualia', *Die Reihe 1*, Pennsylvania, 1958.

Stockhausen, Karlheinz, 'Electronic and instrumental music', *Die Reihe 5*, Pennsylvania, 1961.

Stockhausen, Karlheinz, '. . . how time passes. . .', *Die Reihe 3*, Pennsylvania, 1959.

Stockhausen, Karlheinz, 'Music in space', *Die Reihe 5*, Pennsylvania, 1961.

Stockhausen, Karlheinz, 'Speech and music', *Die Reihe 6*, Pennsylvania, 1964.

Stockhausen, Karlheinz, 'Structure and experimential time', *Die Reihe 2*, Pennsylvania, 1958.

Stockhausen, Karlheinz and others, *Stockhausen in Calcutta*, a commemorative collection of writings selected by Hans-Jürgen Nagel, translated by Sharmila Bose, Calcutta, 1984.

Stravinsky, Igor and Craft, Robert, *Conversations with Igor Stravinsky*, London, 1959.

Tannenbaum, Mya, *Conversations with Stockhausen*, London, 1987.

Vinton, John (ed.) *Dictionary of Twentieth-century Music*, London, 1974.

Wörner, Karl H., *Stockhausen: Life and Work*, revised ed. Bill Hopkins, London, 1973.

Chronological list of works

1952–53	**Kontra-Punkte** for ten instruments	UE12218
1952–53	**Klavierstücke I–IV** for piano	UE12251
1953	**Studie I** electronic music	
1954	**Studie II** electronic music	UE12466
1954–55	**Klavierstücke V–X** for piano	UE13675
1955–56	**Zeitmasze** for five woodwinds	UE12697
1955–57	**Gruppen** for three orchestras	UE13673
1956	**Klavierstück XI** for piano	UE12654
1955–56	**Gesang der Jünglinge** electronic music	
1959	**Zyklus** for a percussionist	UE13186
1959–60	**Carré** for four choirs and orchestras	UE14815
1959	**Refrain** for three players	UE13187
1959–60	**Kontakte** electronic music	UE13678
	version with piano and percussion	UE12426
1961	**Originale** music theatre with **Kontakte**	UE13958
1962–64	**Momente** for soprano, four choirs and thirteen instrumentalists	UE15151
1963	**Plus-Minus** 2 x 7 pages for working out	UE13993
1964	**Mikrophonie I** for tam-tam and six players	UE15138
	'Brussels version' realisation score	UE15139
1964	**Mixtur** for orchestra, sine-wave generators and ring modulators	UE14261
1967	version for smaller ensemble	UE13847

1965	**Mikrophonie II** for twelve singers, Hammond organ, 4 ring modulators and tape	UE15140
1965	**Stop** for orchestra	UE14989
1969	'Paris version'	UE14989
1965–66	**Solo** for melody instrument with feedback	UE14789
1966	**Telemusik** electronic music	UE14807
1966	**Adieu** for wind quintet	UE14877
1966–67	**Hymnen** electronic and concrete music version with soloists	UE15143
1969	version with orchestra	UE15145
1967	**Prozession** for four players	UE14812
1968	**Stimmung** for six vocalists Paris version	UE14805
		UE14805
1968	**Kurzwellen** for six players	UE14806
1968	**Aus den sieben Tagen** fifteen texts for intuitive music (performable individually)	UE14790

    1. **Richtige Dauern** 'Right Durations' for ca. 4 players
    2. **Unbegrenzt** 'Unlimited' for ensemble
    3. **Verbindung** 'Connection' for ensemble
    4. **Treffpunkt** 'Meeting-point' for ensemble
    5. **Nachtmusik** 'Night Music' for ensemble

6. **Abwärts** 'Downwards' for ensemble
7. **Aufwärts** 'Upwards' for ensemble
8. **Oben und Unten** 'Above and Below' (Theatre piece) Man, Woman, Child, 4 instrumentalists
9. **Intensität** 'Intensity' for ensemble
10. **Setz die Segel zur Sonne** 'Set Sail for the Sun' for ensemble
11. **Kommunion** 'Communion' for ensemble
12. **Litanei** 'Litany' for speaker or choir
13. **Es** 'It' for ensemble
14. **Goldstaub** 'Gold Dust' for ensemble
15. **Ankunft** 'Arrival' for speaker or speaking choir

1968	**Spiral** for a soloist with shortwave receiver	UE14957
1969	**Dr. K-Sextett**	UE (hire only)
1969	**Fresco** for four orchestra groups	UE15147
1969–70	**Pole** for two players/singers with short-wave receivers	SV
1969–70	**Expo** for three players/singers with short-wave receivers	SV
1970	**Mantra** for two pianists, percussion and electronic modulation	SV
1968–70	**Für kommende Zeiten** seventeen texts for intuitive music (performable individually)	SV

CHRONOLOGICAL LIST OF WORKS

1. **Übereinstimmung** 'Harmony' for ensemble
2. **Verlängerung** 'Prolongation'
3. **Verkürzung** 'Shortening'
4. **Über die Grenze** 'Across the Boundary' for small ensemble
5. **Kommunikation** 'Communication' for small ensemble
6. **Intervall** 'Interval', piano duo 4-hands
7. **Ausserhalb** 'Outside' for small ensemble
8. **Innerhalb** 'Inside' for small ensemble
9. **Anhalt** 'Halt' for small ensemble
10. **Schwingung** 'Oscillation' for ensemble
11. **Spektren** 'Spectra' for small ensemble
12. **Wellen** 'Waves' for ensemble
13. **Zugvogel** 'Bird of Passage' for ensemble
14. **Vorahnung** 'Presentiment' for 4–7 interpreters
15. **Japan** for ensemble
16. **Wach** 'Awake' for ensemble
17. **Ceylon** for small ensemble

1971	**Sternklang** park music for five groups	SV
1971	**Trans** for orchestra	SV
1972	**Alphabet für Liège** thirteen musical pictures for soloists and duos	SV
	'Am Himmel wandre ich. . .' Indian songs for two voices	

1972	**Ylem** for nineteen players or singers	SV
1973–74	**Inori** for one or two soloists and orchestra	SV
	'Vortrag über HU' 'Lecture on HU' for a singer	
	Musical analysis of INORI	
1974–77	**'Atmen gibt das Leben. . .'** choir opera with orchestra (or tape)	SV
1974	**Herbstmusik** for four players	SV
	'Laub und Regen' closing duet for clarinet and viola	SV
1975	**Musik im Bauch** for six percussionists and music boxes	SV
1975–76	**Tierkreis** twelve melodies for the signs of the Zodiac for a melody and/or chord instrument	SV

1. AQUARIUS
2. PISCES
3. ARIES
4. TAURUS
5. GEMINI
6. CANCER
7. LEO
8. VIRGO
9. LIBRA
10. SCORPIO
11. SAGITTARIUS
12. CAPRICORN   SV

alternative versions for voice and chord instrument

1977	version for chamber orchestra	SV
1975	**Harlekin** for clarinet	SV
1975	**Der kleine Harlekin** for clarinet	SV
1975–77	**Sirius** electronic music and trumpet, soprano, bass clarinet, bass	SV
1977–80	**Aries** for trumpet and electronic music	
1976	**Amour** five pieces for clarinet	SV
	version for flute	
1977	**Jubiläum** for orchestra	SV
1977	**In Freundschaft** for solo player versions for clarinet, flute, recorder, oboe, bassoon, basset horn or bass clarinet, violin, cello, saxophone, horn, trombone.	SV

Cadenzas

1978	Cadenzas for Mozart's Clarinet Concerto in A major KV622	SV
1984–85	Cadenzas for Mozart's Flute Concertos in G major and D major	SV
1984	Cadenza for Leopold Mozart's Trumpet Concerto	SV
1983–85	Cadenzas for Haydn's Trumpet Concerto in E flat major	SV

1977–	**LICHT** **The Seven Days of the Week** **for** **Solo voices, solo instrumentalists, solo dancers,** **choir, orchestra, ballet and mime,** **electronic and concrete music**	

1977	**Der Jahreslauf**
	'The Course of the Years'
	(Scene from Dienstag aus LICHT
	    'Tuesday from LIGHT') for ballet,
	    actor, orchestra and tape or for
	    orchestra alone
		SV

1978–80	**Donnerstag aus LICHT** **Opera in three acts, a greeting and a farewell** **for 14 musical performers** **(3 solo voices, 8 solo instrumentalists, 3 solo dancers)** **choir, orchestra and tapes**

    Donnerstags-Gruss
    Act I: Michaels Jugend
      Kindheit
      Mondeva
      Examen
    Act II: Michaels Reise um die Erde
    Act III: Michaels Heimkehr
    Festival
    Vision
    Donnerstags-Abschied

Individual pieces from Donnerstag aus LICHT for concert performance

1978	**Michaels Reise um die Erde** (Act II) for trumpet and orchestra	SV
	Eingang und Formel (from Michaels Reise) for solo trumpet	SV
	Halt (from Michaels Reise) for trumpet and double-bass	SV
	Kreuzigung (from Michaels Reise) for trumpet, basset-horn (also clarinet), 2 basset-horn, 2 horns, 2 trombones, tuba, electronic organ	SV
	Mission und Himmelfahrt (from Michaels Reise) for trumpet and basset-horn	SV
	Donnerstags-Gruss for eight brass instruments, piano, and three percussionists	SV
	Michaels Ruf for variable ensemble (8 orchestra players)	SV
1978–79	**Michaels Jugend** (Act I) for tenor, soprano, bass; trumpet, basset-horn, trombone, piano; electronic organ; three dancer-mimes; tapes with choir and instruments	SV
	Unsichtbare Chöre for sixteen-track a cappella tape and eight- or two- track playback	SV

Kindheit (Scene 1 of Michaels Jugend)　　　SV
for tenor, soprano, bass; trumpet,
　　　basset-horn, trombone; dancer,
　　　tapes

Tanze Luceva! (from Michaels　　　SV
　　　Jugend)
for basset-horn or bass clarinet

Bijou (from Michaels Jugend)　　　SV
for alto flute and bass clarinet

Mondeva (Scene 2 of Michaels Jugend)　　　SV
for tenor and basset-horn; plus ad lib
　　　soprano, bass, trombone, mime,
　　　electronic organ, two tapes

Examen (Scene 3 of Michaels Jugend)　　　SV
for tenor, trumpet, dancer; basset-horn,
　　　piano; plus ad lib 'jury' (soprano,
　　　bass, two dancer-mimes), two tapes

Klavierstück XII (Examen) for solo　　　SV
　　　piano (from Michaels Jugend)

1978–84　　Version for soloists of Michaels Reise　　　SV
　　　for a trumpeter, 9 other players and
　　　sound projectionist

1980　　**Michaels Heimkehr** (Act III)　　　SV
for tenor, soprano, bass;
trumpet, basset-horn, trombone, two
　　　saxophones, electronic organ;
three dancer-mimes, old woman; choir
　　　and orchestra, tapes

Festival (from Michaels Heimkehr)　　　SV
for tenor, soprano, bass; trumpet,
　　　basset-horn, trombone;

two soprano saxophones; three dancer-
    mimes, old woman;
choir and orchestra; tapes

Drachenkampf (from Michaels   SV
    Heimkehr)
for trumpet, trombone, electric organ
    (or synthesizer), 2 dancers ad lib

Knabenduett (from Michaels   SV
    Heimkehr)
for two soprano saxophones or other
    instruments

Argument (from Michaels Heimkehr)   SV
for tenor, bass, electric organ (or
    synthesizer); ad lib trumpet,
    trombone, percussionist

Vision (from Michaels Heimkehr)   SV
for tenor, trumpet, dancer; Hammond
    organ; tape; plus ad lib shadow
    plays

Donnerstags-Abschied for five   SV
    trumpets (or one trumpet in a
    five-track playback recording)

1981–84   **Samstag aus LICHT**
Opera in a greeting and four scenes
for 13 musical performers
(1 solo voice, 10 solo instrumentalists, 2 solo dancers)
wind orchestra, ballet or mimes, male voice choir, organ

Samstags-Gruss (Luzifer-Gruss)
Scene 1: Luzifers Traum

Scene 2: Kathinkas Gesang als Luzifers
    Requiem
Scene 3: Luzifers Tanz
Scene 4: Luzifers Abschied

Individual pieces from Samstag aus LICHT for concert performance

1981	**Luzifers Traum** (Scene 1) or Piano Piece XIII for bass and piano	SV
	Klavierstück XIII (Luzifers Traum) for solo piano	SV
	Traum-Formel (from Luzifers Traum) for basset-horn	SV
1982	**Luzifers Abschied** (Scene 4) for male choir, organ, seven trombones (live or on tape)	SV

1982–83	**Kathinkas Gesang als Luzifers
	    Requiem** (Scene 2)
	for flute and six percussionists, or flute
	    solo
		SV

	version for flute and electronic music	SV
	version for flute and piano	SV

1983	**Luzifers Tanz** (Scene 3)·
	for bass (or trombone or euphonium),
	    piccolo trumpet,
	piccolo flute; wind orchestra or
	    symphony orchestra; plus
	a stilt-dancer, dancer, ballet or mimes
	    for scenic performance
		SV

Linker Augenbrauentanz (from   SV
    Luzifers Tanz)
for a percussionist, flutes and basset-
    horn(s)

Rechter Augenbrauentanz (from   SV
    Luzifers Tanz)
for a percussionist, clarinets, bass
    clarinets

Linker Augentanz (from Luzifers   SV
    Tanz)
for percussionist and saxophone

Rechter Augentanz (from Luzifers   SV
    Tanz)
for a percussionist, oboes, cors anglais,
    bassoons

Linker Backentanz (from Luzifers   SV
    Tanz)
for a percussionist, trumpets and
    trombones

Rechter Backentanz (from Luzifers   SV
    Tanz)
for a percussionist, trumpets and
    trombones

Nasenflügeltanz (from Luzifers Tanz)   SV
for a percussionist and ad lib electronic
    keyboard instruments

Oberlippentanz ('Protest' from   SV
    Luzifers Tanz)
for solo piccolo trumpet, or for piccolo
    trumpet, trombone or euphonium,
    two percussionists and four or eight
    horns

Zungenspitzentanz (from Luzifers   SV
    Tanz)
for piccolo solo, or for piccolo, ad lib
    dancers, a percussionist and
    euphoniums (or electronic
    keyboard instruments)

Kinntanz (from Luzifers Tanz)   SV
for trombone or euphonium, 2
    percussionists, euphoniums, alto
    trombone(s), baritone (tenor)
    saxhorn(s), bass tuba(s)

1984   **Samstags-Gruss**   SV
for twenty-six brass players and two
    percussionists

1984–88   **Montag aus LICHT**
Opera in three acts, a greeting and a farewell
for 21 musical performers
(14 solo voices, 6 solo instrumentalists, 1 actor)
modern orchestra*

    Montags-Gruss
    Act I: Evas Erstgeburt
    Act II: Evas Zweitgeburt
    Act III: Evas Zauber
    Montags-Abschied

* Modern Orchestra:
electronic keyboard instruments, percussion;
various instrumental ensembles, choir groups, solo voices (recorded on
tape);
8 — track tapes of *concrete* and *electronic sounds*;
40 — channel sound system, 16 — channel sound projection.

Individual pieces from Montag aus LICHT
for concert performance

1984	**Klavierstück XIV** ('Geburtstags-Formel' from Evas Zweitgeburt) for solo piano	SV
1984	**Evas Spiegel** (from Evas Zauber) for basset-horn	SV
	Susani (from Evas Zauber) for basset-horn	SV
1984–85	**Botschaft** (from Evas Zauber) for basset-horn, alto flute, choir, modern orchestra	SV
	versions for basset-horn, alto flute, choir	SV
	or basset-horn, alto flute, modern orchestra	SV
	AVE (from Evas Zauber) for basset-horn and alto flute	SV
1984–86	**Evas Zauber** (Act III) for basset-horn, alto flute and piccolo, choir, children's choir, modern orchestra	SV
1984–87	**Befruchtung mit Klavierstück** (from Evas Zweitgeburt) for piano, girls' choir, modern orchestra	SV
1984–87	**Evas Zweitgeburt** (Act II) for 7 solo boys' voices, solo basset-horn, 3 'bassettinen': 2 basset-horns, 1 voice, piano, choir, girls' choir, modern orchestra	

1984–88	**Montags-Gruss** (Eva-Gruss) for multiple basset-horns, electronic keyboard instruments	SV
1985	**Susanis Echo** (from Evas Zauber) for alto flute	SV
1986	**Evas Lied** (from Evas Zweitgeburt) for 7 solo boys' voices, basset-horn, 3 'bassettinen' (2 basset-horns, 1 voice), modern orchestra, ad lib female choir	SV
	Wochenkreis ('Die sieben Lieder der Tage' from Evas Zweitgeburt) duet for basset-horn and electronic keyboard instruments	SV
	Der Kinderfänger (from Evas Zauber) for alto flute and piccolo, ad lib basset-horn, ad lib children's choir, modern orchestra	SV
	Entführung (from Evas Zauber) for piccolo, ad lib modern orchestra	SV
	Xi for basset-horn (from Montags-Gruss)	SV
	version for alto flute or flute	SV
1987	**Evas Erstgeburt** (Act I) for 3 sopranos, 3 tenors, bass, actor, choir, children's choir, modern orchestra	SV
	Mädchenprozession (from Evas Zweitgeburt)	SV

for girls' choir, ad lib choir, modern
    orchestra

1988   **Montags-Abschied** (Eva-Abschied)   SV
for children's choir, multiple voices and
    piccolos, electronic keyboard
    instruments

Discography

Adieu London Sinfonietta/Stockhausen   DG 2530 443
'Am Himmel wandre ich. . .' (Indianerlieder)
     Hamm-Albrecht, Barkey/Stockhausen   DG 2530 876
Amour Stephens/Stockhausen   CD DG 423 378–2
'Atmen gibt das Leben' (1974)
     NDR chorus/Stockhausen   DG 2530 641
'Atmen gibt das Leben' (1974–77)
     NDR chorus, NDR SO/Stockhausen   DG 410 857–1
Aus den sieben Tagen
     Es-Aufwärts-Kommunion-Intensität-Richtige Dauern-
     Verbindung-Unbegrenzt-Treffpunkt-Nachtmusik-
     Abwärts-Setz die Segel zur Sonne-Goldstaub.

Ensembles/Stockhausen (7 LP)		DG 2720 073
Es-Aufwärts	as above	DG 2530 255
Kommunion-Intensität	as above	DG 2530 256
Goldstaub	as above	DG 410 935–1
Unbegrenzt	same as above	Shandar SR 10 002

     Setz die Segel zur Sonne-Verbindung (different versions)
     Ensembles/Stockhausen   Harmonia Mundi 30 899 M

Setz die Segel zur Sonne Negative Band   Finnadar SR 9009
Setz die Segel zur Sonne Zeitgeist Sound
        Environment Recording Corporation 37662
Carré NDR chorus, NDR SO/
    Kagel, Stockhausen, Markowski, Gielen   DG 137 002
Choral NDR chorus/Stockhausen   DG 2530 641
Chöre für Doris NDR chorus/Stockhausen   DG 2530 641
Dr. K-Sextett Ensemble/Halffter   Universal Edition 15043
Donnerstag aus LICHT
    Various/Eötvös, Stockhausen   (4 LP set) DG 2740 242
        CD DG 473 379–2
Drei Lieder Anderson, SWF SO/Stockhausen   EG 2530 827
Ensemble (Composition studio Kh.S)   Wergo 600 65
Formel SWF SO/Stockhausen   DG 2707 111
Für kommende Zeiten
    Japan-Wach
    Bojé, Caskel, Eötvös (2 LP)   EMI Electrola C 165–02 313/14
    Ceylon-Zugvogel
    Spektren-Kommunikation-Übereinstimmung
        pro musica da camera Thorofon Capella MTH 224
    Ensemble-Stockhausen
        Chrysalis 6307 573 (CHR 1110)/CHY 1110
Gesang der Jünglinge (mono)   DG LP 16 133
    new stereo version (1968)
        Harmonia Mundi DMR 1007–09/DG 138 811
Gruppen WDR SO/
    Stockhausen, Maderna, Gielen
        Opus Musicum 116–118/DG 137 002
    WDR SO/ Stockhausen, Maderna, Boulez
        Harmonia Mundi DMR 1010–12
Harlekin Stephens   DG 2531 006
Hymnen   DG 2707 039
In Freundschaft Stephens/Stockhausen   CD DG 423 378–2
Inori SWF SO/Stockhausen (2 LP)   DG 2707 111
Der Jahreslauf Ensemble/Stockhausen   DG 2531 358

Klavierstücke I–XI Kontarsky (2 LP)   CBS S77 209/32 21 0008
Henck (2 LP)   Wergo 60135/36, Wergo 60135/36–50 (2 CD)
Wambach (2 LP)   Schwann Musica Mundi VMS 1067/68
Klavierstücke I–IV, VII & IX, XI Klein   Point 5028
Klavierstück VI (earlier version) Tudor   Vega C30 A278
Klavierstücke VI, VII, VIII Schroeder   hat ART 2030
Klavierstück VII Bärtschi   Rec Rec Music 04
Damerini   Frequenz 3 DAN
Klavierstück VIII Burge   Vox Candide STGBY 637/31 015
Klavierstück IX Heim   Duchesne DD 6064
Körmendi   Hungaroton SLPX 12569
Letschert
        Musik am Alten Gymnasium Flensberg Fl. 286–48535
Klavierstück X Rzewski
        Wergo 600 10/Hör Zu SHZW 903BL/Heliodor 2 549016
Klavierstücke IX–X Bucquet   Philips TC 6500 101
Klavierstück XI Takahashi   EMI EAA 850 13–15
Der kleine Harlekin Stephens   DG 2531 006
Kontakte electronic music   DG 138 811
Kontakte electronic sounds, piano and percussion
    Tudor, Caskel/Stockhausen   Wergo 600 09
    Kontarsky, Caskel/Stockhausen   Vox Candide CE 31 022
                STGBY 638/Harmonia Mundi DMR 1013–15
Kontra-Punkte Domaine Musical/Boulez   Vega C30 A66
    Ensemble/Maderna   RCA SLD–61 005/VICS 1239
    London Sinfonietta/Stockhausen   DG 2530 443
Kreuzspiel London Sinfonietta/Stockhausen   DG 2530 443
Mantra Alfons and Aloys Kontarsky   DG 2530 208
Mikrophonie I
    Ensemble/Stockhausen   CBS 32 11 0044/S77 230/72 647
    new edition   DG 2530 583
Mikrophonie II WDR chorus/Schernus;
    Kontarsky, Fritsch, Stockhausen
                CBS 32 11 0044/S77 230/72 647
    new edition   DG 2530 583

Mixtur (1964–67)
Ensemble Hudba Dneska/Kupkovic   DG 137 012
Momente (1965) Arroyo, WDR chorus and
Orchestra/Stockhausen   Wergo 600 24/Nonesuch 71 157
(1972) Davy, WDR chorus,
Ensemble Musique Vivante/Stockhausen   DG 2709 055
Musik im Bauch
Percussions de Strasbourg   DG 2530 913
Oberlippentanz M. Stockhausen   Acanta 40.23 543
Opus 1970 (Kurzwellen mit Beethoven)
Ensemble/Stockhausen   DG 139 461
Pole Bojé, Eötvös (2 LP)   EMI Electrola C 165–02 313
Prozession
Ensemble/Stockhausen
     Vox Candide 31 001/STGBY 615/CBS S77 230
(different version)   (Vox)Fratelli Fabbri Editori mm-1098
Version 1971 Ensemble/Stockhausen   DG 2530 582
Punkte (1962) SWF SO/Boulez   DG 0629 030
(1966) NDR SO/Stockhausen   DG 2530 641
Refrain
Kontarsky, Caskel, Kontarsky   Mainstream 5003
Kontarsky, Caskel, Stockhausen   Vox Candide CE 31 022
     STGBY 638/Fratelli Fabbri Editori mm-1098
Schlagtrio Kontarsky, Batigne, Gucht   DG 2530 827
Sirius M. Stockhausen, Meriweather,
Stephens, Carmeli (2 LP)   DG 2707 122
Cancer to Libra from **Sirius** (same recording)
     Harmonia Mundi DMR 1028–30
Spiel SWF SO/Stockhausen   DG 2530 827
Spiral Vetter   Wergo 325/ Hör Zu SHZW 903 BL
Holliger   DG 2561 109
Bojé, Eötvös (two versions) (2 LP)
     EMI Electrola C 165–02 313/14
Sternklang Intermodulation,
Gentle Fire, various artists (2 LP)   Polydor 2612 031

Stimmung Collegium Vokale Cologne   DG 2543 003
new recording 1982, same ensemble
       Harmonia Mundi DMR 1019–21
   Singcircle/Rose   Hyperion A 66115
Studien I und II electronic music   DG LP 16 133
Telemusik electronic music   DG 137 012
Tierkreis (music boxes)   DG 2530 913
   Stephens, Pasveer, M. Stockhausen   Acanta 23 531
   Calame (violin)   Pavane Records ADW 7142
   6-melody version Kremer (violin)
       Ariola-Eurodisc 201 234–405
   6-melody version Rogoff (violin)   CBS/Sony AC 1188–9
Trans (two versions) SWF SO/Bour;
   RSO Saarbrücken/Zender   DG 3530 726
Traum-Formel Stephens/Stockhausen   CD DG 423 378–2
Unsichtbare Chöre WDR chorus, Stephens   DG 419 432–1
       CD DG 419 432–2
Ylem London Sinfonietta/Stockhausen   DG 2530 442
Zeitmasze Domaine Musical/Boulez   Vega C30 A139
   Ensemble/Craft   Philips A 01 488 L/CBS Odyssey 32 160 154
   Danzi Quintett, Holliger   Philips 6 500 261
   London Sinfonietta/Stockhausen   DG 2530 443
Zyklus Caskel   Mainstream 5003
   Neuhaus   Columbia MS 7139
   Caskel, Neuhaus (two versions)
       Wergo 600 10/Heliodor 2 549 016/ Mace S 9091
   Neuhaus (version as Wergo)   Hör Zu SHZW 902 BL
   Gualda   Erato STU 70 603
   Yamaguchi   CBS Sony Japan SONC 16012–I
   Yoshihara, Fry (two versions)   RCA RDC 1
   Yoshihara (as above)   Camerata (Tokyo) CMT 1040
   Fry (as above)   EMI CFP 40207/CFP 40205
Stockhausen Festival of Hits
   Excerpts from: Gesang der Jünglinge, Kontakte, Carré,
   Telemusik, Stimmung, Kurzwellen, Hymnen   DG 139 461

Stockhausen: Greatest Hits
> Excerpts as 'Festival of Hits', also from: Gruppen, 'Es',
> Spiral, Opus 1970, Mantra, 'Aufwärts' (2 LP)
>
> Polydor 2612 023

Stockhausen conducts:

Joseph Haydn: Concerto in E flat major
> for trumpet and orchestra. M. Stockhausen,
> RSO Berlin/Stockhausen   Acanta 40.23 543

W.A. Mozart: Concerto in A major
> for clarinet and orchestra, K.V. 622,
> Stephens, RSO Berlin/Stockhausen   Acanta 23 531

W.A. Mozart: Concerto in G major
> for flute and orchestra, K.V. 313,
> Pasveer, RSO Berlin/Stockhausen   Acanta 40.23 543

Selected films

1 **Musical Forming**   165'
  English   16mm   colour and b/w

2 **Mikrophonie I**   90'
  English   16mm   colour and b/w

3 **Moment-Forming and Integration**   120'
  English   16mm   colour and b/w

4 **Intuitive Music**   60'
  English   16mm   colour and b/w

5 **Questions and Answers on Intuitive Music**   35'
  English   16mm   colour and b/w

6 **Four Criteria of Electronic Music**   105'
  English   16mm   colour and b/w

7 **Questions and Answers on Four Criteria**
  of Electronic Music   105'
  English   16mm   colour and b/w

8 **Telemusic** 60'
English 16mm colour and b/w

9 **Mantra** 120'
English 16mm colour and b/w

10 **Questions and Answers on Mantra** 60'
English 16mm colour and b/w

11 **Momente** 45'51"
English 16mm colour and b/w
French
German

12 **Mikrophonie I** 21'06"
French 35mm and 16mm colour

13 **Stockhausen und die Höhlen von Jeita** 30'
'Stockhausen and the Caves of Jeita'
English 35mm and 16mm colour
French
German

14 **Stockhoven-Beethausen Opus 1970** 49'17"
German 16mm b/w

15 **Ich werde die Töne – die Weltschau
des Karlheinz Stockhausen** 30'44"
'I become the sounds – the world view of Karlheinz Stockhausen'
German 16mm b/w

16 **Internationale Ferienkurse für Neue Musik,
Darmstadt 1970.
Dokumentation einer Misslungenen Revolution** 57'
'International Vacation Courses for New Music, Darmstadt

1970. Documentation of a Failed Revolution'
(excerpts from Stockhausen's seminars 'Feedback'
and 'Expansion of Dynamics')

English	16mm	colour
French		
German		

17 Mantra   56'28"

German	MAZ	colour

18 Mantra   56'28"

English	16mm	colour
French		
German		
Spanish		
Arabic		

19 Trans . . . und so Weiter   58'43"
'Trans . . . and so forth'

	16mm	colour

20 Alphabet für Liège   60'

French	16mm	colour

21 Inori   70'

German	MAZ	colour

22 Inori   82'35"

German	MAZ	colour

23 Inori   ca. 75'

Italian	16mm	colour

24 Michaels Reise um die Erde   ca. 50'

Italian	16mm	colour

25 **'Tuning In' with Stockhausen and Singcircle**   ca. 49'
English   16mm   colour

26 **TG L'UNA**   ca. 20'
Italian   MAZ   colour

27 **Donnerstag aus LICHT im Teatro alla Scala**
'Donnerstag aus LICHT in La Scala'
Italian   16mm   b/w

28 **Notenschlüssel: Stockhausen und seine Kinder**   43'58"
'Keynotes: Stockhausen and his Children'
German   MAZ   colour

29 **Stockhausen und seine Werke**   44'27"
'Stockhausen and his Works'
German   MAZ   colour

30 **Musique et Electronique
avec Karlheinz Stockhausen et George Lewis**   26'
'Music and electronics with Karlheinz Stockhausen
and George Lewis'
French   Video BVU/PAL   colour

31 **Samstag aus LICHT im Teatro alla Scala**
'Samstag aus LICHT in La Scala'
Italian   16mm   colour

32 **Blitz**   ca. 30'
Italian   MAZ   colour

33 **Samstag aus LICHT
– Karlheinz Stockhausens Zweiter Schöpfungstag**   29'45"
'Samstag aus LICHT
– Karlheinz Stockhausen's Second Day of Creation'
German   U-matic   colour

34 **Das Welttheater des Karlheinz Stockhausen**   60'23"
'The World-Theatre of Karlheinz Stockhausen'
German   MAZ   colour

35 **Hymnen mit Solisten und Orchester**   ca. 125'
'Hymnen with soloists and orchestra'
Hungarian   Video SECAM   colour

36 **Kathinkas Gesang de Karlheinz Stockhausen**   33'21"
French   Video BVU/PAL   colour

37 **Donnerstag aus LICHT in Covent Garden**   ca. 45'
English   16mm   colour

38 **Evas Lied**   ca. 42'
German   U-matic   colour

39 **Evas Zauber**   ca. 60'
French   Video BVU/PAL   colour

Addresses

Films 1–10:   Allied Artists, 42 Montpelier Square,
                London SW7
Films 11, 12:   Marie-Noelle Brian, INA GRM, Service
                Diffusion France, Tour mercuriale,
                40 rue Jean Jaurès, F–93170 Bagnolet
Film 13:   MIDEM, 42 Avenue Ste. Foy, F–92 Neuilly

Films 14–16, 33, 34:	Westdeutscher Rundfunk, Fernseh-Musikabteilung, Appellhofplatz 1, D–5000 Köln 1
Films 17, 21, 28, 29:	Werbung in SWF, Produktionsverwertung, Postfach 1115, D–7570 Baden-Baden
Films 11, 18:	German representatives and Goethe Institutes outside West Germany
Film 19:	Alfred Schenz, Neuhauser Strasse 3, D–8000 München 2
Film 20:	RTB, Palais de Congrès, Esplanade d'Europe, B–4000 Liège
Film 22:	ZDF Redaktion Musik I, Essenheimer Landstrasse, D–6500 Mainz 1
Films 23, 24:	Direttore Braun, RTI, via del Babuino 9, I–00100 Roma
Films 25, 37:	BBC, Music Department Television, Yalding House, 156 Great Portland Street, London W1
Films 26, 32:	RAI, Servici segretaria, viale Mazzini 14, I–00195 Roma
Films 27, 31:	Teatro alla Scala, Archivio fotografico, I–20121 Milano
Films 30, 36:	IRCAM/Diffusion, 31 rue Saint-Merri, F–75004 Paris
Film 35:	Magyar Radió Zenei Föosztalya, Bròdy Sàndor uka 5–7, 1800 Budapest, Hungary 0133–039X
Film 38:	Stockhausen-Verlag, D–5067 Kürten
Film 39:	Jean Pierre Lannes, France Régions 3, 14 route de Mirecourt, F–54042 Vandoeuvre, Nancy Cedex

Index

9 780714 529189